LEGAL VISIONARIES

How to Make Their Innovations Work for You

27 INTERVIEWS

David Galbenski

WRITTEN WITH DAVID BARRINGER

2013

Legal Visionaries
©2013 David J. Galbenski
All rights reserved.

Written and edited with David Barringer.
Book design and cover design by David Barringer.
Contact: www.davidbarringer.com.

Printed and bound in the United States.

No part of this work may be used or reproduced in any manner without written permission from the author and publisher, except in the context of reviews.

David J. Galbenski, Esq.
Email: dgalbenski@lumenlegal.com.

Visit www.lumenlegalblog.com to keep up with the latest trends and changes in the industry.

"The world hates change, yet it is the only thing that has brought progress."

—Charles F. Kettering, American engineer and inventor (1876–1958)

CONTENTS

Introduction	7	*Change is Necessary*
Tools for Change	11	*How to Increase Value*
Preface	22	*The 27 Visionaries*

INTERVIEWS

Firoz Dattu	23	AdvanceLaw
Ralph Palumbo	31	Summit Law Group
Elisa Garcia	39	Office Depot, Inc.
Jason Mendelson	45	Foundry Group
Jeffrey Carr	51	FMC Technologies
Richard Munisteri	61	Live Nation Entertainment
Nancy Fraser	65	Med Legal Consulting Source
Mitt Regan	73	Georgetown University Law Center
Josh Linkner	79	Detroit Venture Partners
Ellen Rosenthal	83	Pfizer, Inc.
Michael Roster	91	ACC Value Challenge Steering Committee
Lisa Hart Shepherd	107	Acritas
Matthew K. Fawcett	113	NetApp, Inc.
Michael Baroni	117	Palace Entertainment
Richard A. Matasar	129	New York University
Hugh Totten	139	Valorem Law Group, LLC
Teresa J. Rasmussen	153	Thrivent
William D. Henderson	159	Indiana University Maurer School of Law
Allison Karhnoff	167	Law Graduate, University of Wisconsin
Carrie Hightman	181	NiSource
Richard Susskind	187	Oxford University and Gresham College
Fred H. Bartlit	197	Bartlit Beck Herman Palenchar & Scott
Rodolfo Parga, Jr.	207	Ryley Carlock & Applewhite
Veta T. Richardson	215	Association of Corporate Counsel
Richard Fields	223	Juridica Capital Management, Inc.
David B. Wilkins	231	Harvard Law School
Paul Smith	239	Eversheds LLP

A Note on the Project	249	*About the Authors*

Introduction

PERSPECTIVES FROM ACROSS THE INDUSTRY

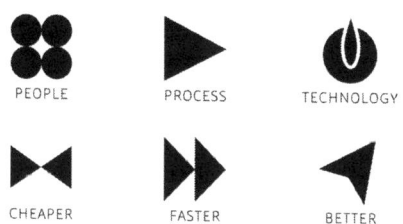

Some legal visionaries advocate measured, incremental steps. Some advocate a willful break from outdated habits. All confront change as necessary.

You can do it, because they already have.

Change comes slowly to the business of law. Everyone knows that. The business of law, however, has changed. In fact, the legal industry changes every year. *Not* everyone knows that. So we put this book together to prove that change is real. Read for yourself.

Good things are happening, and many people are making a difference. The visionaries whose interviews are collected in this book have taken significant steps to improve the business of law. Each person has a slightly different perspective, because each one inhabits a slightly different role in the industry. You will hear from entrepreneurs and a venture capitalist, general counsel and a litigation maverick, law professors and a recent law grad, and many more. Some of them advocate measured, incremental steps. Some advocate a willful break from outdated habits. All of them confront change as necessary. They all appreciate the context of the legal industry within a larger economy that continues to register the effects of global shifts and global pressures. Many people in many industries are, frankly, acting scared. Unpredictability inspires fear in some, and fear inspires a resistance to change. But resisting change is not the way to survive.

Read these interviews, learn from these visionaries, and you will be armed with the tools necessary to start making changes.

You will be the best judge of what changes are relevant and practical, given your current role. You may have the power to make wholesale change, as some general counsel have done. You may have the power to persuade a handful of partners in your firm to break new ground. You may have the power to start your own business, exploiting new opportunities in this changing legal marketplace. No matter what, you will be inspired by the breathtaking scope of what many of these visionaries have already done and what they are planning to do next.

This book, in short, is a call to action. Yes, you may have to engage in what economist Joseph Schumpeter referred to as "creative destruction." What that means to us is that you must destroy the old structure in order to build a new one, break a bad habit in order to learn a better one, and kill off a fearful mindset in order to grow a mindset of possibility and courage. It is far easier to destroy, however, when you have a solid sense of what you are going to create in its place. That is what these interviews can provide: they can paint a picture of what the future can look like. In other words, you can do it, because they already have.

And what have they done? They have brought an entrepreneurial spirit to the business of law. They are constantly thinking about how to do things better, faster, and cheaper. And *cheaper* doesn't mean you sacrifice quality to save a few bucks. It means you consider ways to provide the best value with the most efficient and intelligent means available. In one sense, trying to do things better, faster, and cheaper means that you respect your clients, customers, and colleagues enough to provide the best service, culture, and representation within your means.

If you are interested in improving the business of law, then you bring to bear the mindset of better, faster, and cheaper to three areas: people, process, and technology. The visionaries in this book explain how they have done this. They had the courage to implement change, and they reveal in detail how they went about making those changes. They inspire by example. Learning from their examples, you will pick up the tools, understand the possibilities, and be inspired to action.

To put our motive in simple terms, we set out to collect the good things people are doing in the industry right now, with the goal of inspiring readers with the confidence to take action on their own. Sure, there are always people who complain about the *status quo*. The examples of these visionaries, however, are positive ones: they are making changes, and these changes are overwhelmingly sensible, transformative, and productive.

We identified the major trends in the industry in our previous book *Unbound*, and those trends find continued expression and expansion in this book. The trends are real, but you have to make the effort to take advantage of them. Otherwise, you could end up a victim of them, as the collapse of many major law firms has proven. Those seven trends, in summary, are:

BETTER, FASTER, CHEAPER

+ The demands of business to provide services better, faster and cheaper are forcing the legal industry to behave less like a profession and more like a business.

GLOBALIZATION

+ Globalization is the force that will expand the ways in which legal services are provided to the end consumer.

UNBUNDLED TASKS

+ Tasks will become unbundled, both as a result of business pressures but also as a result of globalization.

CONSOLIDATION

+ Legal-service providers will feel more pressure to consolidate. This consolidation trend will be the result of the new global scale of conducting business.

INFORMATION

+ Consumers and clients know more about legal services than ever before. Information is more available, and the industry is more transparent.

PEOPLE

+ New categories and types of people will be called upon to perform legal services. The demographic composition of the workforce and the attitudes of those working are changing.

EDUCATION

+ There will be new ways to educate legal professionals. Legal education will have to respond to the changing industry.

Those we interviewed for this book have responded in various ways to some of these trends, often according to their own positions within the industry and the scope of the power they have to effect change within their spheres of influence. There is something to be learned from all of them, no matter who you are. An entrepreneur can better understand the perspective of a corporate counsel. A firm lawyer can better understand the perspective of a legal-services entrepreneur. And so on. This broadening of perspective is crucial for anyone in today's world. To make changes, you have to understand the context in which you are making these changes. You have to make the right changes for you, your colleagues, your clients, your customers, your students, and so on.

Where do we go from here? We are excited about the future, and we are excited to hear from you as you, inspired by these visionaries, implement change in your own way. You, in turn, will inspire others around you. They will change, because you did.

Tools for Change

START SOMEWHERE, AND TAKE IT STEP BY STEP

No one in the legal industry has to start from scratch anymore. We can learn from what others have done.

There are many stories in this book. There is a lot of information. There are many points of view, many strategies, and many attitudes. These legal visionaries have made changes, are building on those changes, and are continuing to imagine what they can do next. It's a lot to take in.

You are, of course, free to use this book any way you want. You can find inspiration here and run with it. You can find wisdom here and apply it. We sincerely hope that the interviews we have conducted and edited over the past year and collected in this book will provide you with a wealth of both inspiration and wisdom, as well as knowledge of the current state of change in the industry, understanding of the pressures everyone is under, and evidence of the necessity of making changes one step at a time, starting now.

We also offer the following process for thinking about what to change, how to start, and where to go next.

THE DRIVE TO INCREASE VALUE

The seven trends identified in *Unbound* (see previous chapter) were accelerated by the Great Recession and highlighted the need for transformation and entrepreneurial thinking in legal services. Today, more than ever, the underlying goal for everyone in the industry is to increase the value of the legal services rendered. This drive to increase value is applicable to both law firms (providers) and corporate legal department (purchasers). The most effective way to unlock value in legal services is to utilize a fairly simple framework.

The beauty of the framework is that you don't need to spend hundreds of thousands of dollars in consulting fees to figure out how to take the first steps. You start by identifying your objective for making changes to your current legal-service delivery model. You and your team rank these objectives in order of priority: 1, 2, and 3. The top priority becomes the key outcome you are laser-focused on achieving as you embark on your change process: better, faster or cheaper.

Then you choose which levers you want to use to achieve the desired outcome: people, process, or technology. Again, you and your team rank them in order: 1, 2, and 3. The top priority is the area in which you focus your energies first.

Here are some brief examples.

(a) Focus on *Process* to achieve *Better:* You can improve the quality of your services if you apply Six Sigma methodologies to getting the work completed in the most efficient way possible.

(b) Focus on *People* to achieve *Cheaper:* You can provide services cheaper if you use variable-cost resources instead of fixed-cost resources to perform specific tasks, and you can pass on the labor savings to your clients.

(c) Focus on *Technology* to achieve *Faster:* You can improve the speed of your delivery if you use technology to share information among colleagues, with clients, and even with adversaries and competitors.

You will read about examples like these and more in the interviews with legal visionaries. You can focus on any of the levers of people, process, and technology to achieve improvements in any of the areas of better, faster, and cheaper. But don't think you have to do this all at once! You can't. No one can. That's not the point. The point is to adopt a new mindset, one that embraces continuous improvement over time. With this mindset, you accept that change is necessary, normal, and ongoing. Embracing this attitude doesn't mean you make changes for the sake of change. You make focused changes for the right reasons, one step at a time.

Step 1: Prioritize objectives for seeking change

BETTER	FASTER	CHEAPER
2	3	1

Step 2: Prioritize Levers to Achieve Objective

PEOPLE	PROCESS	TECHNOLOGY
1	2	3

Step 3: align top objective and lever to Manage Change and Increase Value

	BETTER	FASTER	**CHEAPER**
PEOPLE			1
PROCESS			
TECHNOLOGY			

Step 4: Repeat as necessary

THE CAPACITY FOR CHANGE

Most people in the industry understand the need for change, but many don't know how to start. Partly this is due to a perceived gap between where they are today and where they would like to be in the future. How do you bridge that gap? If you can't see from here to there, you begin to overestimate the distance. You picture the first step toward change to be much larger than it is. The gap appears enshrouded in fog, and you worry that there might be a chasm hidden in that fog.

The stories of the legal visionaries will help to dispel much of that fog. By reading about the examples of others, you can start to see the gap between here and there in true proportion. The distance is not nearly as large as it first appeared. The first step is not nearly as dramatic as you worried it might be. And just because there is uncertainty does not mean there is a chasm. It just means you need to do a little research, assess your capacities, and build on small successes.

One of the reasons for prioritizing your objectives is that you don't want to stress the organization's capacity to handle change. You want to make sure everyone understands and prepares for change. That takes time, planning, and good communication. The objective is not change for change's sake. The objective is success. You want to orchestrate a solid achievement and then build on that achievement. So you want to prioritize your objectives and identify one single change with a high probability of success. You want to choose, for example, the lever of *People* so that you can achieve an outcome in the area of *Cheaper*. Success, even small success, boosts the confidence of the members of your organization. Success from a small change will prepare everyone to make another change. And so you choose the lever of *Process* and realize another improvement in the area of *Better*. You build steadily on your successes.

Developing the capacity for change depends on the following two dynamics.

1. Most organizations in legal services have not had to navigate wholesale changes to their operating model. They have not, therefore, had to build up change-management techniques. So integrating simple change-management techniques like those

found in popular business books like *Switch* (2010), by Chip and Dan Heath, into the organization's culture can provide a common vocabulary and change process that can yield great results.

2. The legal industry will continue to change. In fact, many believe change will accelerate. So participants in the legal industry have to adopt a mindset of continuous improvement. That's the process we've been defining in this chapter. The great thing about this framework is that anyone can use it to navigate change. In summary, the stages of this process are:

(A) THE BFC ANALYSIS:

Analyzing and Prioritizing your objectives for Better, Faster, and Cheaper;

(B) THE PPT ANALYSIS:

Analyzing and Prioritizing your levers from People, Process, and Technology; and

(C) THE C^3 PROCESS:

Gain Confidence from the success of others; Build Capacity and Capability to implement Change; and Create a Continuous-improvement mindset in the organization.

WHAT DOES TRANSFORMATION LOOK LIKE?

Entrepreneur: Firoz Dattu started a company, AdvanceLaw, to vet high-performing law firms in order to expand the roster of outside counsel used by corporate legal departments. AdvanceLaw currently works with 19 law firms and 60 companies.

Law firm: Fred Bartlit founded a cutting-edge litigation firm twenty-five years ago. The firm relies on a small team of highly experienced partners who never bill by the hour, rely on communication technology, and share in the outcomes.

Corporate counsel: Ellen Rosenthal is chief counsel for the Pfizer Legal Alliance, which draws on nineteen law firms to create teams of experts on an as-needed basis. Each firm works on an annual flat fee, and the teams are made up of lawyers and staff from multiple firms.

Corporate counsel: Elisa Garcia is general counsel for Office Depot and has developed in-house staff lawyers to provide better service at an affordable cost and deployed a variety of fee arrangements with outside counsel, such as fixed, contingency, risk-sharing, and even combinations of those.

Venture capital: Jason Mendelson is managing director of the Foundry Group. He used the internet to increase transparency in the VC business and created a model-document platform, which decreased cost and increased the speed of delivery. As he puts it, "We raised the transactional IQ of future clients."

Author/Consultant: Richard Susskind advises law firms and legal departments about trends in the legal industry. He has been observing, studying, and writing about the future of law for decades. His predictions about trends in the law are, slowly but surely, coming true, and his clients are racing to take advantage of his advice to survive in the new marketplace.

CHEAPER: PEOPLE > PROCESS > TECHNOLOGY

If you are beginning the initial stages of reviewing your current operating model (say, the traditional law firm), then you, like many in any industry, would likely choose your first goal to be *cheaper*. In the traditional law firm, the value of a lawyer is measured in time. Clients are billed by the hour for the services of a lawyer, whose rate depends not on the value of the work but on the identity of the lawyer providing that work. If you want to provide your clients with the same quality of work but at a lower cost, then you can focus on the people performing that work. Do you have the right people performing each task? Are three inexperienced associates doing a task that should be performed by one experienced partner? Can you unbundle certain tasks so lower-value work can be performed by variable-cost resources instead of fixed-cost associates? Should your operating model move from a pyramid shape to a diamond shape?

Essentially, you are trying to match the value of the work with the value of the person performing that work. You can easily reduce costs if you simply improve this alignment. You don't have highly paid people doing low-cost work, and you don't have three people doing the work of one. If you focus on getting the right people (and the right number of people) doing the right work, then you can achieve your first outcome: *cheaper*.

Let's say you have improved this alignment of value: the right people are doing the right work. And you have achieved some cost savings that you have been able to pass on to your clients. You might then choose another area in which to achieve savings: process. Now, you've already made some advances in the area of process, because, by moving work around to make sure the right people are doing it, you have refined the process of how work gets done. You can, however, continue to focus on process even more.

You might frame your investigation by asking, "Who does what when?" By asking *when* in the process someone does the work, you can find ways to reduce costs. For example, general counsel might participate earlier in the process by sitting in on company meetings they have never been involved with before. By doing so, they might provide advice earlier in a discussion, or they might seek the advice of outside counsel earlier to prevent trouble from brewing. Outside counsel might confer on a more regular basis with their clients for similar reasons: to identify early issues, to prevent missteps, and to provide advice as soon as it is needed. Many corporate counsel have expressed an interest in developing outside counsel as trusted advisors, and to do that, both in-house and outside counsel have to refine the process of how they work together. *When*, in many cases, means *earlier*.

Simply put, by adopting some of the basic fundamentals utilized by Six Sigma professionals or "lean" manufacturing experts, you can discover great improvements to the legal-service delivery model, resulting in increased value for all involved.

And, finally, technology: this is, wisely, the last area in which any outcomes (better, faster, cheaper) should be sought. Technology is often, unfortunately, the first thing people want when confronted with the need to reduce costs, increase the speed of delivery, or improve the quality of services. That is because technology seems easy: you buy it, and it does the work for you.

Often, that can be a costly mistake.

Buying technology before rethinking people and process will simply reinforce existing ways of doing things. New technology on an old business model will simply reinforce all the inefficiencies (all the old valuations) of the old model, if not also create new inefficiencies. So it's critical to pursue new technology only after you have the right people doing the right work at the right time. You must rethink *who* does *what* and *when*. Only then can you think about using technology to improve *how* each person performs their tasks.

FASTER: PEOPLE > PROCESS > TECHNOLOGY

After you have found ways to provide valuable services more cheaply to your clients, you might choose to focus on the next outcome: faster. You again go through the sequence of investigation: who is doing what when and how? In essence, you make sure the right people have the best tools to do their work at the right time.

Maybe you sent some document review to an overseas provider, and that achieved cost-savings. However, you observe that the cost differential between off-shore and on-shore is shrinking, and you need to increase the speed in which that work is done. To do that, you need more convenient oversight. So you move that work to a provider in the U.S. You may pay slightly more, but the oversight is stronger and turnaround is faster. This is called "best-shoring."

Or let's say, in your corporation, your in-house team is handling the review and negotiation of all of your commercial contracts. As might be expected, the complex agreements get first priority while the commodity-type agreements are dealt with when time allows. Often, these NDAs, software-licensing agreements, and vendor agreements are not completed in a timely manner for the internal client. Options exist today to cost-effectively outsource the review and negotiation of the commodity-type agreements to alternative legal-service providers, resulting in both reduced costs and enhanced turnaround time.

BETTER: PEOPLE > PROCESS > TECHNOLOGY

And, as you might guess, these efforts will also have effects in the final desired outcome: better. By making sure the right people are doing the right work with the right tools, you can achieve improvements in cost, speed, and quality. In each area, you are looking to redesign the ways in which people work together. Who is doing what when and how? And because these areas relate to each other—*people* use *technology* to work within a *process*—you can take small steps that lead to big results.

When you think about the issue of *better*, you may find that you need to invest money, time, and energy into achieving this outcome, because, in the long run, you will reap the rewards of this investment. In some legal departments, talent needs to be identified and developed for the legal department in new and innovative ways. Legal departments are now more frequently collaborating with alternative legal-service providers to identify lawyers with subject-matter expertise to provide on-going services to the corporation in a "secondment" capacity. Due to the changing demographics of the lawyer population, a burgeoning pool of experienced lawyers is available on demand; these are lawyers who have previously served as partners at prestigious law firms or corporate counsel at some of the world's largest corporations. It may be cheaper to employ on-demand, experienced lawyers as needed rather than adding permanent headcount inside the corporate legal department, and it is certainly cheaper that the traditional law-firm rate structure. But the impetus for drawing on the talents of this pool of experienced attorneys is not about cost-savings: it's about improving the value of the role a particular attorney can play for their client. It's about *better*.

The effort to find better ways to do things is going on not just in the context of law firms and legal departments, but in the larger context of the industry. We find law firms consolidating to address the needs of their global corporate clients. We find new legal-services providers starting from scratch to capitalize on the trends of unbundling, best-shoring, legal staffing, and legal self-help. We find law schools trying to adapt legal education to the changing marketplace. We find legal associations like the Association of Corporate Counsel bringing discussions of value in legal services to the forefront of the industry. We even find countries like Australia and the UK changing regulations governing the legal industry in order to open up new operating models. We find institutions, universities, corporations, entrepreneurs, and innovators working to do things *better*.

SMALL STEPS > BIG RESULTS

You can drive value by trying to do things better, faster, and cheaper, and you can make those things happen by making changes in people, process and technology. This framework is relatively straightforward, intuitive, and actionable immediately. However, our experience is that the legal industry is stuck at the third and final step of this framework, the step we call "C^3." Ultimately, that step is where all the value is created. So get moving. You can start by taking small steps. These small steps, taken over time, will transform the way you do business, whether you are a general counsel in a legal department, a lawyer in a law firm, or an entrepreneur in a legal-services company.

A CAUTION

Since the highest cost of providing legal services is in the people, and most organizations are looking to unlock value by getting the work done cheaper, the first lever most people attempt to utilize is to move from a fixed-cost model to a variable-cost model. Then organizations address how the work is getting done (process) and apply technology to accelerate each step of the process of delivering legal services. Organizations, however, quickly run into trouble when they try to execute a game plan on all three (people, process, technology) at once. It is more effective to start by focusing on one area, make changes in that area, review the results, and then move on to the next step.

LEARN FROM LEGAL VISIONARIES

Before you take the first step, however, you want to get the lay of the land. You want to do some research. You will grow comfortable with making changes only after you see what others have done. What tools have been tried? What strategies have delivered results? That's where this book comes in. This book provides you with a view of the landscape. Read what these visionaries have to say, and you will be able to look before you leap. You will have the benefit of their wisdom, born of their experience, before you take your own measured step toward transformation.

Preface

THE INTERVIEWS

The following legal visionaries hail from a variety of backgrounds and industries. They are general counsel, entrepreneurs, partners, professors, leaders, investors, and innovators. With all of them, we discussed the past, present, and future.

Regarding the past, we asked what changes, if any, they had made in response to the Great Recession. Many of them had already instituted changes and were prepared for the drastically altered economic landscape. They did not endure the same dramatic convulsions that others did in the industry. That was not too surprising. Acting in anticipation of changing trends is precisely what makes many of them visionaries.

As for the present, we asked many of them similar questions, such as:

+ How do you define value?
+ How do you deal with pricing?
+ How are you developing your operating model?

You will be able to compare what many of them say about these recurrent and important topics. However, we also let the conversations go their own ways. Everyone has a different experience with innovation, and everyone is at a slightly different stage and brings a slightly different perspective. So we let the visionaries report on what they were doing at the moment and what was important to them now and in the near term.

Finally, we asked about the future. We asked about what trends they saw on the horizon, what new strategies they were about to embrace, what direction legal education might take, and even what advice they might give to current legal graduates.

We trust these interviews with legal visionaries will give you a sense of the big picture of today's developments and tomorrow's trends, as well as provide a deep and rich view into what tools these visionaries are using to achieve big results.

Firoz Dattu

CEO
ADVANCELAW
ARLINGTON, VA

"The partners under our model have the incentive to overperform, because they know they're being evaluated, and a positive evaluation will bring more business from a large group of potential clients."

Is it a good idea for young people today to get degrees in both business and law?

It's certainly helpful. An MBA will introduce you to accounting, business models, finance, and microeconomics, and that helps in so many contexts, including law. I think that, traditionally, lawyers have been insulated from training in management, communication, and leadership. That said, business school isn't the only place to develop all these skills. I have, in the past, led mini-MBA courses for in-house lawyers, and I'm sure resources providing that training are still out there. Law schools are gradually changing to try to develop well-rounded, business-minded lawyers. Harvard, for example, is increasingly incorporating the business of law into its curriculum.

Somewhat related to this issue of business training, law firms too are gradually improving in terms of training their lawyers to focus on business outcomes and not only legal outcomes. Most law firms still have a ways to go. The managing partner of a large firm recently noted there is a generational difference at law firms in which the newer partners are aiming to change the practice of law to be business-focused, while many of the seasoned partners simply aren't capable of thinking of law in that way.

Is having experience working in a law firm crucial to becoming a legal entrepreneur today?

I may be biased a bit, because I was at a law firm and left after just a couple of years (even though it was a firm for which I have a lot of respect). In a nutshell, I think law-firm experience gives an entrepreneur helpful context and credibility, but it's not crucial. People listen to good ideas, regardless of the background of the person, and I'm finding that as we move from a pure profession to more of a business, prospective clients and customers look to non-lawyers' fresh perspectives. Even the practice of law (not just being an entrepreneur in the legal field) seems to be managed increasingly by non-lawyers, as regulations regarding who can own or manage a law firm are relaxing over time. And lawyers aren't necessarily the people who will drive change in the legal market, given that cross-professional experience is so helpful and lawyers have historically not always been the best managers.

When was AdvanceLaw launched?

AdvanceLaw officially launched in February of 2010. I was finding that GCs were frustrated by the rising billing rates at large firms, and they were even more frustrated by the lack of efficiency. GCs also knew that talent was not just at the AmLaw 20 or the Magic Circle firms, but they didn't know which firms and partners to trust if they were to migrate work away from the incumbent or pedigreed firms. It's a scary thing for an in-house lawyer to move work to a new firm with which they don't have experience. That was the role I envisioned AdvanceLaw could play: provide assurance to GCs when they try out a new firm or lawyer. Simply put, it's not reliable enough to receive suggestions from colleagues or legal directories. AdvanceLaw provides GC participants with the service of law-firm vetting and encourages law firms to provide the top lawyers to these GCs and then motivates those lawyers to excel (on quality and efficiency).

What does AdvanceLaw do?

AdvanceLaw identifies law firms in the US and around the world that understand that quality and efficiency are not mutually exclusive. We are currently working with 19 such law firms in 25 countries. The 60 large companies with which we work have access to the 6,500 lawyers at these 19 firms, each committed to striving for the AdvanceLaw GCs. The law firms excel for these GCs because we share our evaluation data across the GCs. Essentially, this is a way for a law firm (and specifically a partner on a matter) to impress an entire network of GCs on the basis of strong performance. This is what's missing in the legal market—accountability for performance. Normally, if a law-firm partner does a "so-so" job for an in-house lawyer, there may not even be a dip in that partner's revenue, because that in-house lawyer may not be inclined to switch firms (at least not right away), and rarely does the dissatisfied in-house lawyer inform a large group of potential clients about the less-than-stellar experience. That's the problem AdvanceLaw addresses. The partners under our model have the incentive to overperform, because they know they're being evaluated, and a positive evaluation will bring more business from a large group of potential clients. In this way, we encourage and reward exceptional performance for AdvanceLaw GCs.

What is your role in AdvanceLaw?

I do a bit of everything at AdvanceLaw, just like all entrepreneurs, I would guess! Two years ago, AdvanceLaw was a one-person shop, but today, we have a truly amazing team of five individuals. So I am focused on strategy. That said, I will always be involved in all aspects of AdvanceLaw, and my vision is not to grow too large. Client service is absolutely critical for me, and I'd rather have a business that exceeds our clients' expectations than a business that loses its focus and quality. And for AdvanceLaw, it's not all about financial gain. I and everyone on my team are passionate about making the legal market more efficient for GCs and rewarding the good lawyers out there who impress their clients. I'd like to stay lean, and so I will always be involved in all facets of the organization. I think many entrepreneurs try to grow too quickly through external funding, but that's not appealing for me. I want to grow carefully and make sure that our reputation for client service stays intact.

Were you positioning yourself for a long time for your current role launching AdvanceLaw?

As much as career-planning is a good idea, it's amazing how much our careers take shape organically, each step a logical extension of our last experience. When I went to law school, I thought I'd be a courtroom lawyer. As a child, I'd watched *Perry Mason* TV shows and movies. I wasn't so sure about that after I had an internship while in law school at the DA's office. I went to work in a law firm working on all kinds of litigation (including a *pro bono* case defending a death-row inmate). While some of the work was thrilling, I found that so much of it involved paperwork and details. And that's more the reason I left the law for business. I went to an organization called the Corporate Executive Board where I helped launch a group for GCs called the General Counsel Roundtable—giving them management and strategy advice. Through the GC relationships and industry connections that I formed, I was able to get AdvanceLaw off the ground. It takes the trust of a group of GCs to back something new like this, and I was lucky to have that. And then the original group of GCs had good experiences and success stories through AdvanceLaw, and they started recommending other GCs for me to invite into the group. That's what is making this project succeed, even more than any career or business plan I had. At this point, we are lucky to have such a strong network of blue-chip companies and amazing law firms really committed to excellence, and a lot of this I would chalk up simply to good fortune, one career move at a time.

What are some of the success stories?

The GCs have been remarkably positive about their experiences with AdvanceLaw firms, and we've seen many relationships evolve as a result of outstanding performance. For example, a $5 billion company sent several hundred major product-liability matters to an AdvanceLaw firm and is very happy with the performance received. A $50 billion company is using AdvanceLaw in the IP area and finds that the firms it retained are especially practical and responsive.

To me, however, some of the best successes are where we came through on a short time frame—for instance, helping the GC of a $60 billion company find, within twenty-four hours, the legal help he urgently needed for internal investigations taking place in multiple cities. I can't help but feel lucky to hear sophisticated GCs speak about our business model as helpful to them. One of them, from a roughly $100 billion company, noted that "other ways of selecting outside counsel just don't have the reliability and level of insight as AdvanceLaw." Another, from a $5 billion company, said publicly, "You know, AdvanceLaw did their homework, and you can trust their conclusions." I don't mention these successes out of bravado, but I want to point out that GC successes and value are how we measure our success.

How do firms get into AdvanceLaw?

I seek to identify firms that embrace partnership with GCs to achieve business goals, have high quality standards and customer-service ethic, can deliver on efficiency, have a commitment to diversity, and are more than willing to experiment with alternative-fee arrangements.

To identify firms with these attributes, I use a rigorous and detailed vetting survey, and I follow that up with interviews of law-firm partners, associates, clients, and various GCs I trust and respect. I knew that finding the right law firms was imperative to AdvanceLaw's success and, more importantly, ability to provide outstanding service to our group of GCs. Several law-firm partners have commented that this was the toughest RFP or selection process they had ever experienced. They also told us we asked the right questions, and we earned credibility through the process.

We continue to add firms to the AdvanceLaw network, both domestically and internationally. We are working with 19 firms in 25 countries. Companies are growing globally at a quick pace, and the legal department has to keep up. Finding great counsel for, say, consumer-protection issues in Europe or an acquisition in Argentina is a challenge, and we can confidently and quickly provide leads for our GCs and their teams to consider. And we can provide motivation for the firms and partners to perform well.

How do you manage the working relationship between the clients and the firms?

With the law firms, we work closely to ensure the attorneys understand the importance of doing their best work for AdvanceLaw GCs—that they will be evaluated and the feedback shared across a larger group of potential clients.

And by collecting feedback from in-house lawyers on past and ongoing matters, we know which firms and partners are performing particularly well, and we get a sense of what can be improved. Our goal is to communicate back to the law firms whatever we can, while preserving GC confidences. The act of communicating to a firm or partner where they are appreciated by clients and where clients feel they could improve is more than enough to change and improve behaviors. In fact, we find law firms are keen for this feedback. And because the law firms and partners know that strong success helps them, they are conscientious about improving. The firms have been receiving high grades from the GCs from the outset, but it's interesting that the scores are getting even higher over time, perhaps because of the feedback we are providing. And for their part, the GCs completely understand the value of making the legal market efficient and of receiving strong evaluation data, so they and their teams are keen to provide their feedback.

What kind of feedback have you been getting?

The feedback has been overwhelmingly positive about AdvanceLaw firms. We consistently hear the firms' lawyers are responsive, business-focused, and have the relevant expertise to efficiently provide high-quality work. Also, the GCs appreciate the reliability of the AdvanceLaw network. One GC said he had "little to no anxiety" about choosing counsel in new locations anymore, after his experience with us, and another mentioned "improved peace of mind." I feel like we're doing our job when a GC says, "This lawyer knocked it out of the park, and before this, the firm wasn't even on my radar."

How are the AdvanceLaw firms responding to the demands from GCs?

The firms are eager to respond to market requirements. Law firms are working to transform themselves from a group of independent professionals to a team of business partners. They are changing billing structures and, in some cases, compensation plans in order to better align with client needs.

How do you monitor how well the AdvanceLaw firms are performing for their clients?

Our evaluation process for each matter gives us a good data set to rely upon. Additionally, every two years the firms are required to resubmit an RFP to continue to be a part of AdvanceLaw. And we are not shy about having conversations with in-house lawyers to hear about their experiences.

The ratings across all evaluations on 1–5 scale are over 4.5 on expertise, quality, responsiveness, and cost. So the partners are taking the matters seriously, and the incentives seem to be working.

Honest feedback frequently doesn't happen between in-house and outside counsel, either because there is no mechanism for it or the conversation is too awkward. We are in a unique position to hear and communicate honest feedback to help the firms improve their performance.

What trends do you see in the industry?

Recently, I asked 30 GCs of Fortune 500 companies and 13 managing partners of major law firms to rank a list of trends according to likelihood of occurrence, and the significant ones are: (1) GCs will migrate a larger percent of work away from "white shoe firms," creating opportunities for a new set of firms; (2) more efficient, non-traditional legal-service providers will emerge, spurring all law firms to innovate; (3) the allure of being a panel law firm will decrease, as GCs are sending work outside their panels often through RFPs for major matters or portfolios; (4) there will be more and better data on the performance of specific outside counsel; and (5) alternative-fee arrangements will increase over time.

Ralph Palumbo
Summit Law Group, PLLC
Seattle, WA

"Our idea was to dramatically reduce overhead and share part of the benefit with our customers."

When did Summit Law Group start?
We started about sixteen years ago. I was here in the beginning. A group split from a larger firm, because we wanted to start a new operating model, which we did, with Summit. Most of the new things we started doing have proved successful in producing what we wanted them to produce. Over the years, a lot of firms have adopted a number of our practices, or at least they say they have.

Did you do anything differently in the wake of the 2008–09 recession?
We had already made a lot of changes. We'd moved to the lowest possible overhead structure we could. I thought it made no sense for a professional firm to have a profit margin in the 35% range. I thought that was upside down. I thought there was something dramatically wrong with law firms taking home that profit percentage when they should be taking home 65 or 66 cents out of a dollar. And it was clear to me that law firms were spending overhead

dollars in ways that did not contribute to the success of the work they were performing for customers. Our idea was to dramatically reduce overhead and share part of the benefit with our customers. Without making any real sacrifices, we cut overhead from 65% at our former law firm to 35% at Summit. When the financial crisis happened, we had a greater ability to maintain profitability. We had almost no bump at all in 2008 and 2009. In 2010, we were down a little bit. It was not a good year. But 2011 was one of our most profitable years.

How do you hire?

We don't hire out of law schools, so we don't have this continuing talent pool. We identify people who have been successful after four or five years of practice.

I've become somewhat ambivalent about whether or not we should hire out of law school. You can miss talented people out of law school who end up at firms where they stay. You need certain attributes to succeed in school and other attributes to succeed in practice. You take lawyers with the best records at the best law schools, and there's a high probability they'll be highly competent. But a small cohort has other attributes that translate into being successful private practitioners. Some were average students but exceptional lawyers. We don't have a year-in, year-out need to hire two to three people. We have the luxury of hiring people with experience.

Some of our lawyers have become client counsel or even CEOs. We're entering a phase in which we're looking at lateral hires to strengthen the firm in certain categories. We're looking to identify lawyers in their middle and late thirties and forties who are successful and on a path to greater success. We're in a more aggressive stance in terms of growing the firm than we've been in a while.

What is the training like for new lawyers at Summit?

We have adopted a horizontal approach to handling client matters. We have several lawyers working on a matter, and there's no hierarchy among the lawyers. We divide up the brief, and each of us writes a portion. We don't have a junior lawyer write the brief and then pass it up the line for editing by more experienced lawyers. We allow everyone to participate at all levels. It permits us to put more talent on matters. It's more time efficient. By operating in that way, we don't need any training program other than what our young lawyers get by working with other, more experienced lawyers in our firm. I learned by watching and working with other talented lawyers. So I try to teach other lawyers now. I say, "Here's what worked for me, and you have to figure out what works for you." It's constant training, and that's really the way lawyers progress in the profession. Taking a school deposition is no substitute for sitting with me and taking a real deposition.

You write, "Some people, even some people at Summit, perceive Summit's egalitarian practices as being motivated by 'quality of life' issues. It is important to understand that every change we made at Summit was made for a business purpose—to improve profitability by improving customer satisfaction." Do you think firms are slow to change because they're ingrained in habit or because they devalue this kind of change as wishy-washy and touchy-feely?

This has been an issue. We have been looking at our practice and business development, and we had an outside firm come in to conduct interviews with our lawyers and staff. (The surveys were confidential.) Roughly 20% of our lawyers and staff view their work at Summit as just a job. It's a challenge to practice the way we do and at the same time heavily involve the staff in firm activities, meetings, and decisions. We try to give flexibility to our young lawyers and in particular our young women lawyers, because their talent is valuable, and we want our efforts to be perceived as business efforts rather than motivated by pure quality-of-life efforts. We do these things to make us more profitable. We involve the staff in everything we do because we know that gives us a more committed staff. We get great ideas from staff. Lawyers do not have a monopoly on good ideas about how a good firm should function. We encourage staff involvement to capture the creativity of legal professionals to make us more profitable. Our flexibility in accommodating female lawyers who wish to balance career and family has made us an attractive firm for the best female lawyers. We have highly successful women lawyers because we attract the best female lawyers who want this flexibility. It's a major advantage we have over other firms, and it makes us profitable. We're small, and we have the ability to say, "If you want to come here, you should want to accomplish something extraordinary, and that's going to require a higher level of commitment. And you're not going to get this kind of working relationship somewhere else."

One of your Summit Core Values is: "To create and maintain a law firm in which all lawyers and staff have an entrepreneurial stake in the enterprise." What is this entrepreneurial stake?

Our compensation system rewards hard work individually by lawyers and staff. We pay close attention to each lawyer's net collected contribution to the firm. We don't track who necessarily bills the matter. We track who is a major contributor to generating the work and maintaining the relationship with the client. Our philosophy is that the more people we can have in direct relationship with customers, the stronger our relationships will be. If I have a significant client, I want to operate with that client so that not only do they have a direct relationship with me but also with all lawyers working on the case, as well as with paralegals, the billing department, my legal assistant, etc. We value client relationship and development. We think that gives us greater success with customers and stronger relationships. I have customers who regard the paralegals working on the matter as every bit as valuable in the relationship as the lawyers.

We do quarterly bonuses based on firm performance and annual bonuses based on the firm's work and business development. And whenever we have a highly successful year or when we receive a big contingency fee that year, our awards to the staff are disproportionate to what other firms do. Our staff has in the past received bonuses of 50% of their salary. A staff member making $80,000 a year may receive, in an especially good year, a bonus of $20,000 to $40,000. Our philosophy is that by handsomely rewarding staff, we are able to hire the best and retain the best. That translates into profitability, because we are thinly staffed compared to large firms. When we started with twelve lawyers, we had about seven staff members. Usually staff outnumbers lawyers in big firms. So we have staff members who do the jobs of what three to four staff members do in other big firms.

We never want to have non-lawyer staff doing the same job in a serial, redundant way. We want their work to be challenging and imaginative. We staff lawyers on matters so we're doing something once. If I edit a portion of a brief written by a younger lawyer, I'll send it back to them to accept or decline my red lines (or talk to me). By the same token, I might write different sections, and they'll edit my work. We have drafts, and we look at each other's drafts. If I read a draft that's not written the way I would want, I try hard not to interfere and rewrite the draft in my own voice. I only change the writing if it really matters to the customer or a judge, not just to get it to read in my own voice. Lawyers have a tendency to rewrite briefs written by another lawyer in their own voice. It's expensive to do that, and we don't do it.

How would you describe your operating model?

I think the most effective thing we've done in terms of keeping our model fresh—and these things are invisible and not terribly well noticed even by our lawyers and staff—is that we very purposely have minimum possible oversight on what our lawyers and staff do in the day-to-day practice. When someone wants to buy a laptop or iPad or cellphone, they don't have to get permission to do that. If someone wants to vary how they bill a client a little bit, you would in other firms have to chase approval. But you don't have to do that at Summit. We trust our lawyers and staff to make decisions about what's best for customers and Summit. Just do it. If you make a mistake, then don't do it anymore. To paraphrase Tom Peters, "If you want to be innovative, you have to learn how to make your mistakes faster." I believe that's right. If you don't unleash the good judgment of your lawyers and staff, then you're not going to keep things fresh, and you're going to keep doing stupid stuff. The challenge is not to constrain your staff from doing things they shouldn't be doing. The challenge is to free them up to believe we trust them and to get them to do good things we never would have thought of.

Have you adopted any new ideas or practices generated by your staff and lawyers?

Yes. In the pricing area, our policy is that if you come up with a new way to price with the customer, then do it. The young people have come up with ways to use Twitter, for example, to keep up with customers. That comes from the younger people, not from my generation. Over the past fifteen years, we've had lots of contributions from staff to keep our model and practices up to date and responsive. Everyone takes this seriously. A couple years ago, someone on staff was talking about a late-night brief or a big project, and two to three other legal assistants stayed until midnight to help this person out. They coined the phrase, "The Summit team runs toward the fire." If I'm doing something that requires a late-night effort, I don't have to go to anyone to get permission for help and work and support from others. Another person who doesn't have anything on the case will run to the project to help out. That happens every single day. The staff sees a problem someone else has, and they run to the problem to help out. This stuff just happens. It's one of the things I'm most proud of.

Many years ago, someone sent an email thanking other people for helping. No one officially adopted the practice, but somebody did it, and it was rewarded, and now whenever someone does something they should be congratulated for, someone sends an email to everyone in the firm praising the efforts of that person to everyone else in the firm. Those emails fly around Summit on a daily basis. That has the impact of encouraging supportive behavior and making it part of the way Summit operates.

How do you handle pricing?

One thing to mention that troubles me that I don't have an answer for: we have tried to constrain the level and growth of hourly fees. We tend to be at the low end of the market in terms of the amounts of our hourly fees. And we don't automatically increase our fees every year. But there remains a perception that if a lawyer costs more, they must be better. Some of our outside marketing firms tell us to raise our rates because keeping them low damages the reputation of our lawyers. We don't keep our hourly fees low just to stay less expensive. We do it because it enables us to have several senior lawyers contributing their work to the same matter. Anything we bill is going to be somewhat smaller than a comparable team from a large firm, but our team is likely to have more senior people on the team. To do that and remain competitive, we've kept our fees down. But there persists the perception in client community that high rates mean high quality.

I don't know what to do about that. I'm reluctant to raise our rates, because many of our clients like them. I thought a larger percentage of corporate counsel would recognize that the lawyers they're hiring at small boutique firms have attended the same law schools and have the same experiences as those in big expensive firms. There are still a lot of corporate counsel in major companies who hire lawyers from big firms in part because they can't be criticized for hiring big firms in New York and DC. It's a challenge for us.

Big firms can't get away from fact that they have to have higher rates to support the greater overhead of running thousand-lawyer firms. Big firms have all the different kinds of lawyers a big company needs, and that's a reason to go to one of those firms. But there are plenty of things we can do as well or better. In my observation, corporate counsel are more willing to take their litigation work to smaller specialty firms than they are to take their corporate/commercial work to smaller specialty firms.

What do you see for Summit in the next five years?
A trend for Summit in the next five years is to grow so that we achieve a greater critical mass in our corporate group, environmental group, and litigation group in particular. We want to compete in the market with bigger firms. Our labor group has done this.

One thing I'd like to accomplish before I retire is I'd like to work on evaluating pricing. I want to have pricing structures in which we're rewarded beyond the hourly rate when we've had great success. Success comes with good fortune, good facts, and good outcomes, and we also share the downside with customers. The challenge is to get the customer community to engage. It's comfortable to do hourly-based billing and contingency fees. It's a tough thing to get the overall client community to change to pricing most of the work on a value basis as opposed to an hourly basis. That's why I have such admiration for what Bartlit Beck has managed to accomplish in that area, because everything they do is value-based billing.

It's one of my goals, but I'm pessimistic about accomplishing it in the next ten years of my career. I think it's good for us and good for the client. We always stay open with the client in alternative-fee relationships to monitor how it's going during the matter and the case. It's easy to go into the office and count hours. It's totally different to go into the office and say, "I've got to be successful." Once you make that switch, you come up with all sorts of new ways to make success happen.

Elisa Garcia

EXECUTIVE VICE PRESIDENT &
GENERAL COUNSEL
OFFICE DEPOT, INC.
DELRAY BEACH, FL

"We talked as a team about how we could do the work in-house better, cheaper and smarter. We also reached out to our law-firm partners and talked about how to restructure work around a value proposition."

How did you get involved with the Association of Corporate Counsel (ACC)?

When I joined Domino's Pizza, a board member from the ACC in Michigan reached out to me. I went to a meeting, and I met a number of GCs from auto manufacturers, insurance companies, distributors, etc. It was such a rich place, a place of ideas, with people always exchanging information. For someone like me, a New York lawyer moving to Michigan without any experience with the local firms, I got a wealth of information and connections. People were truly willing to help. I eventually became president of the Michigan chapter, so for seven years in Michigan, I was very active. When I moved to Florida to join Office Depot, I was asked to join the ACC's national board. This is a stellar group of attorneys who have accomplished so much and are singularly focused on serving the in-house bar, whether through defending the rights of in-house counsel, or training them, or offering them networking opportunities. I co-chair the steering committee for the ACC Value Challenge, which motivates GCs to ask what kind of value they're getting out of their law firms.

How did you respond to the financial crisis of 2008?

I had just recently joined Office Depot. I'd been there only a year when the financial crisis hit. My first year, I put out fires. It wasn't until the fall of 2008 that I began to really understand the business and how the legal department could be better integrated into it. There had been a division between litigation and corporate legal work with a VP heading each team. We had the opportunity to restructure the legal team by having our functional experts (contracts, labor and employment, litigation, real estate) report to one deputy GC, and through that, we were able to provide greater integration among areas affecting our day-to-day business. For example, we had been reviewing documents for certain legal provisions, but we weren't getting involved early in the contract-negotiation process, where we could offer the business some real value. After the restructuring, there was greater information-sharing, and litigators now oversee some contract review, and business lawyers attend business staff meetings and provide strategic guidance on matters that could expose the company to litigation risk. We are much more integrated into the business.

From 2009 and into 2011, we continued to restructure the law department, and we grew, in fact. We added a contract-compliance function, brought more IP experience in-house, and added some government-relations experience to our team. The more lawyers we added, the greater value the client was receiving. This was measured in reduced outside legal fees. Our internal lawyers, after a brief training period, provided greater value than outside law firms could. With or without the recession, I would have looked at my department, but I doubt we would have been able to hire the caliber of lawyers that we were able to at that time. We hired lawyers away from great law firms.

How did you find these lawyers?

Often we had a relationship with the firm, and we knew the lawyer. They'd done work for us. For the most part, when we want to hire a lawyer from a firm, the firm supports our decision. It strengthens the relationship, though they may gripe a bit. Some firms had made too many commitments to promising young law-school graduates in 2009 to 2010. We were the beneficiary of one firm "giving" us the services of a first-year lawyer whom they did not have sufficient work for. This was tremendous help during a financially difficult time for us and for the firm. The young lawyer received great insights into in-house practice and front-line experience, and now that she is at the firm full-time, she has had the kind of client exposure that a seventh-year associate has not even received.

How long did the restructuring take?

It took about a year. We changed the way we worked, and we realized we needed more lawyers to do the work we created.

Is demand up?

Our major customer is small business, and the small-business sector is, statistically, the slowest to get back on its feet. When home-equity lines dried up, which tended to be the money people used to start businesses, our business suffered. They've started to come back, but Office Depot sales have declined for three years. About forty-percent of our revenue comes from retail stores, 30% from international, and the other 30% from the business-solutions division (a direct-selling arrangement with business clients, state or local governments, or school systems). The contract business has grown, but this business has relatively low margins, while the small-business owner who buys through the retail store has shrunk his demand. Business continues to be difficult, in part due to the economy, but also because of the changes in our sector (fewer computers being purchased, decreased use of paper, ink and toner).

How did you start thinking about restructuring the law department and the work done by outside firms?

It really began with the departure of one of the lawyers in the department. This was a great opportunity to step back and look at how we worked. I also had my prior experience at Domino's Pizza. I brought with me what I'd learned. I wasn't necessarily looking at the GE or DuPont model. The ACC began providing resources on the ACC Value Challenge around the same time we were looking at our work. Using this information and reviewing the law-firm models, we talked as a team about how we could do the work in-house better, cheaper and smarter. We also reached out to our law-firm partners and talked about how to restructure work around a value proposition and utilize alternative-fee arrangements when we could.

What were some of those law firms doing differently that you liked?

After we determined how to best serve our client, we looked at how to get better value from our outside law firms. We had to find ways to do our work more efficiently and at a lower overall cost. We looked beyond the billable hour, for example. At least 40% of our outside legal spend is done on an alternative-fee basis.

What alternative arrangements work best for you?

We use a number of different arrangements. In single-plaintiff labor matters, we have utilized a fixed fee up to summary judgment and another fixed fee for the trial. This year we are negotiating a fixed fee for all of our employment litigation. In litigation, we have used contingency-fee arrangements and joint defense groups in patent litigation to reduce fees. We've also done risk-sharing. For example, we pay at 60% of the hourly rate, and we "hold back" the remaining 40%, which the firm can earn as a performance bonus. We've also done flat fee with shared savings. The firm tracks their hours, and we agree, let's say, to $100,000 for a particular matter. If they spend more than that, we get it for that flat fee. If they do it for $80,000, they've made an extra $20,000. However, if they do the work for $50,000, then we made a mistake in pricing, and we'll share the savings. They'll give us $25,000 off the next fee arrangement. It's a two-way trust arrangement, which is helpful with firms that haven't done alternative fees. Firms are doing their best to price their work, but they have to share information after the fact, so there's a trust factor. Sometimes it's hard for a firm to convince some of their partners to do alternative fees. My CFO loves the idea that we have greater predictability with flat fees. Firms who have been doing this for years for certain cases have become very good at managing these matters. If we find an alternative fee is not working, we renegotiate.

Do GCs have larger roles today in demanding change from their legal service providers?

Absolutely. However, the extent of my involvement depends on the matter. In a large merger-and-acquisitions deal or litigation, I'd get more involved. I want to understand staffing, meet the lawyers, ensure diversity on the team, know whether or not any work is being outsourced to India and to which outfit, and so on. If a firm has an in-house, low-cost provider for document review, I want to understand these dynamics.

I think a greater role for the in-house legal team is evolving, especially in document review. We had a large SEC investigation with huge document production, and we established a direct relationship with a third-party, document-review company instead of the law firm's document-review team.

How do you think about value in legal services?

With our in-house lawyers, I see them as preventative medicine: they're in the business of being in staff meetings with our business unit partners. We provide training. We're involved early in deals, and we provide value in evaluating risks and things to think about and work around.

It's trickier educating in-house lawyers about how to get value from outside lawyers. Most of our in-house lawyers are trained in the billable hour, and that's how they know how to work. They have to rethink how to find "value" and how to price it in a lawsuit. For a dismissal at summary judgment, that's great, and I'm willing to pay X dollars. They've never thought about it that way. We've used the TyMetrix billing system, and that really helps us analyze the costs of matters by type and by stage. We can pull all employment matters up to summary judgment for years, and we'll know the average cost of a matter. We can come up with a fair price we're willing to pay, and everyone makes money. This is not something taught in law school and not necessarily understood by firms.

We recently created a new position in the department. We have our own IT manager, a paralegal good at managing data and pulling reports and putting that information into a form we can use. We're becoming a lot more like every other department in the company. In the past, lawyers hid behind the mystique of the law, but the economic crisis has focused CFOs as much, if not more, on the legal department than on others.

Does that make your life difficult?
It makes it easier for me to drive change in the department. They understand we have to do things more efficiently, just like every other department has had to become more efficient. We've grown, while every other department here has had cuts. This is only because by bringing on more heads we have been able to save money. And our legal team knows we've become more efficient using data, and so they've become very conscious of data and its importance.

Something very important to me is *pro bono* work, and it was not part of the culture of the department, although some lawyers did work on their own. It took a couple of years, but the team is now involved and excited about *pro bono* legal work and community service. We had a representative from a legal-aid society come in and do training in foreclosure mediation and representing children, and now we're tracking our *pro bono* and publishing the hours we spend on it. We have also found community projects to involve the entire department, not just the lawyers.

What trends do you see in the next three to five years?
I think we're going to see smaller and midsize firms specialize and become more successful. I think the law is becoming more commoditized, and I'd be more likely to go to specialty firms for employment or class-action matters, because they will have the data and experience to break down the case into tasks. They'll know what the tasks are going to cost them, they'll share that information with me, and we'll work to find the best price. I think smaller firms will be better able to work with their clients this way, and I welcome it, because it will make my costs more predictable.

Jason Mendelson

MANAGING DIRECTOR
FOUNDRY GROUP
BOULDER, CO

"Historically, clients have felt powerless to insist on change, but now the Internet has changed that. We can share documents, experiences, billable hours, and how any firm prices and values work. It's become the client's duty to change the system."

What is the Foundry Group?
I am a co-founder and managing director of Foundry Group, and we're based in Boulder, Colorado. We're a venture-capital firm, and we invest in early-stage, information-technology companies.

What kinds of companies are you investing in?
We invest in themes. Most VCs invest in sectors. You picked up from our website that we have an interest in companies working on human/computer interaction. On that particular theme, we've invested in Makerbot, Fitbit, Modular Robotics, Sifteo, Organic Motion, and many others. Check out the company Oblong.com.

These guys have developed the real version of the kind of technology you'd see in the movie *Minority Report*. They've come up with a 3D operating environment. These guys can move 3D data within a room or a collaborative environment. If you were typing something, you could throw it to me on my screen, and the actual data set would show up here with me. It's the idea of opening up the computer interface into the spatial environment. It's done and it works, and in the next year or two, they may be able to bring it to the consumer level. Big systems are at big companies. Their first mass-market product is called Mezzanine, which is a collaboration system that sits on top of Cisco's Telepresence. But we have a half dozen other themes that we invest in as well.

Did you change anything business-wise during the 2008–2009 crisis?

In 2007, I was writing blog posts predicting the crash in the legal industry, and the legal journals just hammered me. You can check out some of those entries online at jasonmendelson.com. I had just become so fed up as a venture-capital client. My first blog was about how most lawyers who worked with start-ups frustrated me. The reaction was sudden: start-up lawyers called and offered me fixed-fee deals, even law firms worried they were the subject of my rant. One blog post probably saved us $100,000, if you add up what we saved in legal fees investing in companies, and they all know that I'm that guy who wrote the blog posts demystifying term sheets and venture-capital financing. People ask, and I say, "Yeah, I'm *that* guy." My portfolio companies love it.

It's not that I'm a pie-in-the-sky client. I was at big law firms and a big company for eight years. So I know all the inefficiencies. When I was general counsel at Mobius, we were getting sick and tired of paying top dollar and getting the same documents from law firms, so we were part of several firms that started a model-documents initiative within the NVCA. In 2000, when I had just started at Mobius, I was paying $30,000 to $40,000 to get any financing work done, and it made no sense, because early-stage financing is all similar, a degree away from each other. With the model-document platform, we forced law firms to become more efficient, and now I have deals getting done for $15,000. The price has gone down dramatically.

Did you put pressure on how they priced the work or on how they did the work?

Both. We open-sourced the documents at the NVCA website. My partner and I wrote blogs exposing the tricks about term sheets which eventually turned into our book *Venture Deals*, and that was all about how you do deals to cut down on inflated prices and inefficient processes. In the old days, lawyers said, "Trust me," and we'd hammer each other. Now entrepreneurs are calling up VCs and agreeing on 80% of what needs to be done, and we let the lawyers handle the rest of it. And there's no black box that hides who is getting charged for what and why.

How exactly were the document templates open-sourced?

We posted them online, publicly. We had approximately 30 law firms and 20 VC funds, and we posted all that on the NVCA website.

And the reaction was...?

The reaction was outstanding. Between that and the blog that my partner Brad and I wrote on all the tricks of the term sheets, it was very well received. It's the reason we got the book deal from Wiley Publishers. We know of about 35 business schools using our blog and/or book in their courses. We raised the transactional IQ of future clients. We tried to whittle down the redundancies of what lawyers were charging their clients to do. In the old days, if I were investing $500,000 in a company financing, the lawyers were taking 10%. For what? It made no sense. Lawyers wouldn't change, so we changed it for them.

That theme comes up a lot: that change has to come from clients and corporate counsel.

When I jumped the chasm from being a lawyer to being a business guy, I realized that attorneys focused on revenue and hours, but they are blind when it comes to thinking about margins. And margin is profit. They make as much revenue as they can, and a couple of guys at the firm figure out the profit. Most firms are run by folks who can't adapt to be financially efficient, so it falls completely on clients to force any change. Historically, clients have felt powerless to insist on change, but now the Internet has changed that. We can share documents, experiences, billable hours, and how any firm prices and values work. It's become the client's duty to change the system.

How long did you practice as a lawyer?

I started as a lawyer in 1998. I left the law firm Cooley Godward Kronish in 2000, and at Mobius, I practiced as a lawyer through 2006. During 2003 and 2004, I started to work on the business side as well, and now I spend about 2% of my time working in the law and 98% in business.

Why did you make this switch from law to business?

My change from law to business was very gradual. I'm one of the few lawyers who did not want to be a VC. As a law student, I just wasn't interested. It didn't seem very interesting. I started taking on more deal work and just ran out of time to be a lawyer. Intellectually, I still find the law more interesting than some of the work of being a VC, but I don't like the practice of law. I don't have to bill time as a VC, and I help companies because I want to. Also it's nice to be in a field where you get to help folks with all of your working hours, not adverse to them, as some situations in the law.

How do you think about value in legal services?

To the client, the lawyer's judgment is the key. Many corporate lawyers have their judgment beaten out of them. They become so risk-averse they don't want to make a judgment call. Corporate lawyers also have the view that what they do is not that important, and the work is rote. Having been on both sides of the fence, I think that's wrong. There are tons of legal judgment calls that greatly affect business. Less than 15% of lawyers are highly skilled balancing risk and judgment, in my opinion.

At most law firms, nothing's changed. Value is still measured by time—meaning, by revenue, which is driven by hourly billing. Inside a big firm, it's always about how many hours you bill, and that's what you're paid. Smaller firms are starting to value other things, like public presence and business generation. Some big clients will pay for that reputation. So any real changes in the operating models are happening at small firms. There is some change happening in the mid-sized firms finally, and that's working its way up. The less pricing power you have, the more you're willing to change how you're doing business.

Look ahead three to five years, and talk about the significant trends relevant to your business and the legal industry.

One is technology. We've invested in Brightleaf.com, which is creating an automated legal-documentation platform. Some of the IT work is getting outsourced overseas, like patents and prior art and due diligence. There's more hiring of contract attorneys while still billing clients at higher hourly rates. Wages are going to go down. Firms with an upper echelon of partners are trying to stay the same, however, for the moment.

What kind of a marketplace are law graduates entering today?

Many students coming out of law school are screwed. The price of law school is tracking to the billing rates of partners, and the problem is clients aren't paying for junior lawyers anymore. Now law school is $40,000 a year or more! A student graduates with $150,000 of debt. What can they do? How can they pay that back when salaries aren't rising to keep up?

Do you miss anything about practicing law?

I don't have a gravy train like I had when I worked at the law firm, where a *C* can get you a good career. In the VC world, you perform or you get nothing.

You even made a Youtube video about being a VC. Why did you make that video, and what was the reaction to it?

It's called "I'm a VC." Just search Google for it. It's Justin Timberlake's *Saturday Night Live* videos meets venture capital. The reaction was great, except for a few VCs who thought we denigrated the profession. That made me very happy to hear. The entrepreneurs loved it.

You are also a drummer. Any way I can hear you play?

Yes! The latest album is for my band Legitimate Front, and the album is *Off the Hook*. It's on all the streaming services, iTunes, Amazon, etc. It's a '70s-styled album with all original music. My business partner Ryan is the lead guitar player. I'm the drummer and singer.

Jeffrey Carr

V.P., General Counsel & Secretary
FMC Technologies, Inc.
Houston, TX

"An advocate helps you when you're in trouble, but the best role for an in-house lawyer is to be a counselor who helps clients stay out of trouble."

Your name often comes up as a good example of a general counsel pushing for change.

I live out there in the radical extreme, but it's not quite as lonely anymore and not quite as extreme.

How do you think of your role in today's marketplace?

Our mission statement starts out with, "We are not lawyers. We are people with legal training." Our own lawyers didn't like it when we drew it up because we are, of course, lawyers. The point is that we are not lawyers in the way most people are used to thinking about lawyers. We help our client company manage risk and achieve their business objectives while maintaining their ethical compass. As a lawyer, you have to step back and ask if what you're doing is truly helping your client. Of course, we have to maintain an ethical compass. We have to be focused on that all the time. We are not in the business of answering interesting questions of law or even, for that matter, "winning" disputes. We are in the business of making and selling oil-field equipment and services, and the client really doesn't care what the answer is to a question of law that you find interesting. We care, but clients typically don't. The client just needs to know that the area of risk is being managed and that they're making progress in achieving their objectives.

How do you deal with pricing?

We have to deliver right-sized legal services for the company to achieve its objectives. I run a high-performance legal team. We have eleven lawyers globally, but we have other people on our team: outside counsel, non-lawyers, consultants, experts, support staff, and others. Last year, our total inside and outside legal spend was less than $10 million—which is significantly below benchmarks for manufacturing companies of our size. We achieve that by being on the front end of things. It takes more work to be a pro-active counselor. Most law firms adhere to the business model of billing hours for putting out fires. Firms, and indeed most lawyers whether inside or outside, love to fight fires. There's urgency and drama. It's an adrenalin rush, and it creates more hours to bill. But our clients pay for results, not hours.

Do you ever deal with hourly billing?

We do almost 100% of our billing based on performance. We started this back in the Nineties. Lawyers tend to think business stuff is for administrators and accountants to worry about. They don't like thinking about it. They'd rather think about the law and all of the interesting questions that are posed. Firms are generally built on a foundation requiring maximization of hours; hence, lawyers tend to focus on effort as a way to achieve results as opposed to efficiency as well as effectiveness. But part of our job as in-house lawyers is to be managers of people and resources and money. Every million dollars that the legal team can save the company by avoiding costs, reducing fees, or bringing in money in licensing result in a measurable boost in shareholder value by increasing our earnings per share.

How do you balance in-house staff with external firms?

We use a "make or buy" process for all that we do. At one level, I look at inside and outside counsel as the same; it's just a question of whether they get paid by a paycheck or through an invoice. In either case, they are on the FMC Technologies legal team, and I don't really care who their partners are or where they work. What I care about is whether we're working as a team. It's almost always cheaper to use inside than outside resources, but it's generally not possible or efficient to try to staff for peaks in work, for all expertise, and for processes and procedures that are extremely time-consuming. An example is litigation, which we aren't going to try to fully staff from internal resources. We manage litigation, but we run it from the strategy side. I can't afford to have a staff of litigators and send them wherever they need to go.

I reduce our legal spend to the smallest percentage of revenue possible. We run at about .18% of revenue, which is astounding for the size of our company. We are a $4.5 billion company. We have manufacturing globally. We deal with highly sophisticated goods and products. We formed the legal team in 1991. The company has grown from $1.8 billion to $4.5 billion in revenue, and our legal spend has been flat for that period. We focus on processes and procedures to standardize work where we can. We use the right tools and avoid problems as opposed to fighting fires. An advocate helps you when you're in trouble, but the best role for an in-house lawyer is to be a counselor who helps clients stay out of trouble. The cost of damage control is high. The investment in risk prevention on the front end is not. In other words, pro-active lawyering can substantially reduce the overall legal costs incurred by a company.

Are GCs taking on more active roles today?

We have taken a more active role. We push to find efficiencies. We don't micromanage our counsel for how they do what we've engaged them to do. We don't use legal-process outsourcing here, but we encourage our firms to do that. We just don't have the staff to manage an LPO network to send work out to India and so on. It's an issue of capacity and allocation of very scarce resources, not cost. We don't tell firms what tools to use, but we're going to give incentives to reduce costs and increase their profit margin. We want the firm to be profitable, but based on efficiency and margin as opposed to top-line revenue growth. We hope to unleash an entrepreneurial spirit in the law firm. We don't have this long list of things not to bill us for. We address it the opposite way. The cost has to be all in and include everything. I could care less where you sit on an airplane or how you ship something. It doesn't change the price I pay. If I tell them they can bill me for telephone time, in a world in which phone calls are almost free, there is no incentive for the firm to do anything other than to pass that cost to me. The firm can find a way to reduce that cost. They can use Google or other free services as opposed to Lexis and Westlaw. As clients, we're not going to pay for that cost. They have to figure it out. So we still use economics to do it.

How do you define value?

I'm very involved in the ACC Value Challenge. People define value differently. I define it simply and have a definition that works for pretty much anything. Value is helping us achieve whatever our result is effectively and efficiently. It's not a function of hours. It's a function of effectiveness and efficiency, and you can measure this stuff. The fascinating thing in legal services is that every lawyer will tell you every case or deal is different, but if you look at the data statistically, it's a bell curve. You can plot costs, and you end up with a bell curve. There will be outliers high and low, but there's always a cluster of data. You ought to take that as the target, as the mean, and you should try to get savings of a standard deviation every year or five years, whatever the repeatability is. It's amazing, the more you look at the data, the more you realize how the rules of normal distribution always apply. You have specialists who will make money at that specialty, if they can, but that doesn't mean the client should pay for inefficiency. Most work that companies need is basic blocking and tackling. So to pay a premium for that work is insane.

Do you use a flexible-team kind of model, staffing up and down on a project basis, as needed?

Yes, we use what I'd call the Hollywood-staffing model. For any given project, you may have five people you go to: for gaffers, best boys, or adverse-possession cases. You may not get your first choice. That's okay, because most people are relatively fungible in these roles. So why pay a premium to "reserve" capacity you may or may not ever need? You need to have flexibility. I believe in assembling teams of people who are right for the job. It takes more effort, because this model runs right into the issue of dealing with large egos and a law firm's view of self-worth.

We're dealing with that in litigation. A few years ago, we looked at changing our panel of litigation firms. We invited the world to respond to a non-RFP. The first step of the non-RFP was composed of thirteen questions that had to be answered yes or no. Then we gave them one page to tell us what made their firm different. The second stage dealt with numbers. We gave them our data for types of matters, and we asked for their data on contracts, injury cases, etc. The third and last stage was a two-hour meet and greet, but first they had to send me a Tweet to persuade me that I should take two hours out of my day and my team's day and spend it with them in a *wow* not *woo* meeting.

We thought we were going to find a few firms that were heads above everyone else. We found the opposite. A couple of firms were interesting, but these were largely outside our industry or our geography. On the other hand, there were a bunch of firms we sort of liked. We formed a joint venture with these firms, and when a new piece of litigation comes in, we form a litigation team from these six firms. The case may need one lawyer or twenty. So it's possible that one firm or several may be involved in any given matter. We've done this, and it's been an interesting experiment. But, frankly, we haven't had more than few new cases to test this version of the Hollywood-staffing concept fully.

How have the firms liked the arrangement?

One time, an outside lawyer put his arm around me, a cigar in his hand, and said, "You are my least significant but most important client." When I think about that statement, it occurs to me that's precisely what every GC should aspire to. We only use performance-based pay, so we push firms to be better and different. We gladly market for those that excel. We tell other companies about how good our firms are. We want them to make more money per hour than they would in a normal billing scenario. We just don't want to buy as many hours, but we'll help them sell that extra inventory of hours. If we can help them be more productive, they can sell more and make more. So that's our deal with law firms. We think we can help firms be better businesses.

What types of firms have been more responsive to pressure to change?

Firms fall in three camps, in my opinion. Some large firms are like medieval castles, with walls tall and thick. You can never frontally assault a castle. You surround and starve it. So we don't work with them. The second camp consists of firms and lawyers who are interested in changing, and we focus on working with these people. They wake up wondering how to do this work better, faster, and cheaper. They ask, "How can I help FMC get this deal done today?" Once we find these lawyers, we nurture them. The third camp, in contrast, plays lip service to value billing and new service models, but they don't mean it, because life is good for them. Why change?

So a segment of the market will be able to price their work at a premium. Certain law firms working for financial markets, for example, may be relatively insulated, because legal costs represent such a small percentage of the overall fees and costs to the customer for these financial services. Other firms—generally smaller boutique firms with particularly or significantly different cost structures or niche-type specialties should continue to prosper, so long as those niche products and services are in demand. But those in the middle tier, if they're not innovative, will die. Folks who choose to become innovative will survive and prosper. The GC community has to lead by example. We're the customer. Too many in-house lawyers simply don't feel that their job is to deliver shareholder value. GCs had to start telling their staff lawyers to change, and, if they don't change, then the GCs will find someone who will. GCs need to use performance-based pay both internally and externally to make this happen.

At some point in the next few years, resistant law firms and GCs will wake up to find they have become irrelevant. They'll find that they have worked themselves out of business by failing to address what clients need.

Has anyone tried to replicate your system?

Some firms do use our system. They've pitched it to Company X and Y, and while some firms have been very successful, the answer they get is often, "It sounds good, but let's try it next time." And tomorrow never comes. This debate has been raging in the legal press for eons. We lawyers will debate forever and never do the simple thing, which is just go test it out. Change will come when the CEO walks into the GC's office, throws down a *Wall Street Journal* or *Fortune* about us, Cisco, Pfizer, or some other innovative legal team, and asks, "Why aren't you doing this?"

Will new graduates and young lawyers accept change faster?

The downsizing of "big law" and the surfeit of lawyers on the market, while exacting a huge human cost, may well be the salvation of our profession. Maybe some of these folks will find new jobs in new platforms that are being created. New graduates may be the best hope. Maybe they will form completely different kinds of legal-service providers using newly available capital models and information-technology models.

They don't have that legacy investment—they don't care whether the old models die out, because they can't get jobs within those models anyway—and so maybe they will be desperate and free to try something new.

There is, for example, Legal Zoom. They have more customer recognition than any law firm, and it's this form process, an incorporation package for $99 or whatever. The Walmarts of the world will provide legal resources needed by, appropriate for, and right-priced for consumer and small-business legal needs. Then you have firms like Clearspire and Axiom, the latter of which had one of best taglines ever: "Pay for what's in a lawyer's head, not what's over it." They have an interesting model, but it's not interesting enough. They took the partnership structure out but still provide legal services on a drastically reduced hourly billing rate. It's a start, but it's not fundamentally changing the model.

There are other people focusing on back-office improvements, on automating process and content, and on standardizing products and services. I know young people will fit in, but they're not going to make $160,000 a year anymore. As a customer, I know there is not a first-year associate on the face of the Earth worth $160,000 to me. I stood up and said that to an audience. I said, "They don't know anything that is useful to me." And I said if associates are reviewing documents for discovery, well, I can get that done by someone else at a fraction of the cost.

Ultimately, changing the model requires leveraging technology and work product to streamline the production of process and content and letting lawyers work on the higher value areas where their judgment actually does come into play. This isn't rocket science. Most legal needs are, in fact, quite susceptible to standardization and commoditization. The unique application of professional judgment to a set of facts is where things get dicey. This is and should be the province of lawyers—in other words, advocacy and counseling, the areas where a lawyer's professional judgment comes into play. That's where lawyers are uniquely capable and should be used. In areas of legal process and content? No, not so much.

Can people come out of law school today and find new kind of roles—new kinds of jobs—for the legally educated?

People flow out of law school with debt and romantic ideals. The problem we face is a creative disequilibrium as we move in this transition to what some people call the "new normal." What happens to the sixty-year-old lawyer who is used to doing things the traditional way? What about the twenty-two-year-old law graduate who expects $120,000 a year to pay off school loans?

I have this working understanding in which I consider legal services falling into four buckets: process, advocacy, counseling, and content. Lawyers provide process and counseling, and those provide the most number of hours. Advocacy can be composed of negotiation, litigation, and lobbying. Counseling is proactive. Advocacy is reactive. Today in the industry, we have a law-firm infrastructure built on process and content, and I think we're moving toward a world where content is relatively free and process grows more important. We're going to need true project managers, and we won't need lawyers to do a lot of the process—that is, if my view of the world is correct. I don't know for sure that it is.

In today's world, we have too many lawyers being paid too much money. The lawyers don't want to give it up, and the new folks, understandably, don't want to make less money either. So what do people do in this transition? In a day-to-day sense, I don't have time to care. I focus on how we continue to work our model our way.

What criteria are important to you when hiring lawyers?
The interesting thing about lawyers is they all think they're unique and the best, but frankly, most legal work is highly standardized. It's specialized within certain areas, and it can be commoditized. Quality today is not a differentiator; it's the price of admission. We make hiring decisions based on culture and fit. We don't really care where the person clerked or went to law school. I need people capable of providing counsel based on good, sound legal judgments. I don't really need great legal thinkers capable of pondering and answering interesting questions of law.

Are GCs sharing their new systems with other GCs to inspire them to make similar changes?
GCs are bonding together to do things better, faster, and cheaper. We are figuring out ways to build our own new systems. The in-house community today is so much tighter than it was thirty years ago. Back then, many thought the in-house crowd was comprised of martini-swilling guys who couldn't get work elsewhere. While I really don't share that view as historically accurate, I know that today, I sit with the CEO and the CFO, so I'm damn sure that I'm cost-accountable and results-accountable. I'm damn sure my team delivers on both scores, not just one. The GCs are closer to realizing they're the customer. We're starting to work smarter, and we talk among ourselves more and more. There are only a couple thousand GCs in the world, and we're getting to know each other. We talk about what we're doing and what works—and what doesn't. We exchange information about LSPs and firms. Information platforms have enabled us to collaborate easily. There's a new generation of law-department leaders, and we're far more business-oriented.

Richard Munisteri

SENIOR VICE PRESIDENT,
ASSOCIATE GENERAL COUNSEL
LIVE NATION ENTERTAINMENT, INC.
BEVERLY HILLS, CA

"We've had an outside agency track and provide metrics on our cases so we can compare what we'd pay under the traditional model of using a law firm with what we'd pay using new models."

Have you made any changes in response to changes in the industry?

In terms of the economy, we seem at times to be inversely related to what's going on in the rest of country. We had good years in 2008 and 2009. We had a drop in 2010. This might have had more to do with artists' ability or inability to perform shows or tours. We're not really affected by the legal industry. We had cutbacks in late 2010 as a result of overall performance for that year. We have a higher level of scrutiny on cost for outside legal matters, particularly discovery costs and review costs.

I would say, before 2007—even during the years when Live Nation had a parent company that was overseeing litigation matters and activities like large-scale document review—the advent of large-scale electronic discovery and production really didn't hit. In 2007, we had a good learning experience organizing a matter with a combination of outside counsel and contract staffing. We not only staffed all activities in the matter through outside counsel but also assembled contract staff to perform all necessary activities that didn't require the specialized expertise of outside counsel. From that experience, we realized the way litigation was going.

What did the work involve?

We had a large-scale, e-document review and document production, which cost a lot of money, so we used contract staffing. The idea was a necessity when we looked at the numbers. With the volume of work we had, we were going to need 30 to 40 attorneys, and the rates we'd pay a firm would be astronomical. So rather than paying $300 to $400 an hour, you can have contract staff do it for $40 to $50 an hour. The way e-discovery has evolved, it's become a more regular occurrence. Before then, we relied on the traditional model of outside law firms doing everything. From our experience, we didn't know any better, but, thankfully, we had not had a major document-review project come about yet in which the numbers made it imperative that we explore other options.

Why didn't you know any better?

We hadn't done the work to compare cost-savings. We had not, by then, had a lot of big cases involving major electronic-document review. We only had a handful. Since that time, we've had an outside agency track and provide metrics on our cases so we can compare what we'd pay under the traditional model of using a law firm with what we'd pay using new models. In one project, the savings over the life of the project was $5.5 million.

Has using new models changed your relationship with law firms?

It has. And also, for litigation matters, we've changed our approach to the extent we use contract staffing or other legal-service providers. Some law firms have turned around. Some of them still put up road blocks when you use contract staff, because that takes work from them, but they realize we're their client. In the past, firms had said we could use contract staffing for the first pass, but for quality control, we needed to have firms do the final review. So I went along with that, but then it occurred to me I was paying twice for the same work. It was too much money. I said it didn't make sense. There are a lot of highly qualified, highly skilled attorneys who are between jobs or out of work, especially with the economy, and they're doing contract work to fill gaps in their careers. If you have that talent available, I saw no reason to pay a law firm exponentially more. So we started using contract attorneys more, doing both first and second pass reviews, and even getting them more involved in privilege-review aspects of the project.

What trends have you noticed in the industry?

One trend that has my attention is that the client has better mechanisms to track productivity in real time. Historically, the in-house counsel or client contact had to travel to different parts of the country to be physically present and monitor the work the outside counsel was doing. I haven't been able to do this, so I appreciate that now they bring it to the in-house attorney's desk. I have the ability to pull up a dashboard on the computer, sign into a project, and see what they're doing, what they're looking at, and what they've been working on. The technology allows me to do my job, but I can monitor progress from my desk, so I don't have to travel all over the country.

What kind of pressures are you under in your job today?

I'm busy. There's a reason the company pays my salary. On top of my normal job duties, every day I've got a parade of vendors knocking on my door or ringing my phone—around ten per day, usually—and I have to set aside time for that, because there is some value in knowing what's going on out in the marketplace and which firms offer what. I'm working in an area where there's a regular need to contact with all sorts of providers. Keeping up with trends in industry can be taxing on my time. So I don't feel it's necessary for frequent client-contact and in-person visits, but occasionally it's good. What speaks to me in the area of contract-attorney staffing is, "Are we getting qualified reviewers assembled timely and sent out to complete the project," and "Is there a very attractive price associated with it?" That's what means the most to me. I want to see and monitor activity, get reviewers to the site, have a way to track productivity, and head off mishaps before they happen.

How do you define value?

It's a matter of controlling the bleed. For document review and production, you need to find the thing that hurts you and will be part of the case, and with email and electronic documents, there's now so much to go through. The value of e-discovery has gone up, because you have to go through this mountain of crap to make sure there's not a "gotcha" moment in there somewhere. Cost is the main driver in managing legal matters, and traditionally, a lot of the work of review is a waste of money. So there's value in making the review more efficient. You want to control price without sacrificing quality, and you need a combination of technology and good reviewers and mechanisms for tracking to be successful at catching the documents that help us, or hurt us, in our case.

How do you manage contracts for talent?

We have in-house lawyers for contracts. We have thousands of contracts each year, and there are templates for use in the field, for certain deals. But several reasons may push a contract into our in-house department for review. For example, for a global touring agreement with a major artist, we may have a team of attorneys work on various aspects of the deal for months. But for the small-dollar booking of a niche act for a single night at a local club, then usually that level of contracting does not warrant complete involvement of the legal department, absent some special circumstance.

Nancy Fraser

FOUNDER AND CEO
MED LEGAL CONSULTING SOURCE
LOS ANGELES, CA

"We've unbundled each service, so we have the right people doing the right jobs. We assign teams case by case. We have a multilevel process to ensure quality, and our people work remotely and virtually."

What does Med Legal do?

We have three service lines: medical-record analysis, audit, and life-care planning. We perform medical-record reviews for insurance companies, plaintiffs, law firms, etc. We use a network of contract nurses combined with process technology. We have ten full-time staff in Los Angeles and about seventy or so subcontractors, which include nurses, coders, paralegal editors, and life-care planners. Operations include four full-timers who manage all this. Once the records arrive, they manage them, assign teams, track workflow and deadlines, and move them through the process to final case review and outtake.

Life-care planning is about planning for future medical care costs or needs. For example, if someone suffered an injury, a big part of the case is what future medical care they'll need for rest of their life. We create a line of care and associate cost with that plan. We factor in life expectancy, and it ends up being a single figure taking all medical needs into consideration. We're the only company that bundles these three service lines together.

How does this work in practice?

We believe everything is done better in teams. Everyone functions at higher and more efficient capacity. In a company with three service lines, we have professionals for each service, like those who create reports, who perform audits, as well as certified life-care planners. We've unbundled each service, so we have the right people doing the right jobs. We assign teams case by case. Whatever the case involves, we pull teams together. We have a multilevel process to ensure quality, and our people work remotely and virtually.

For quality control and review purposes, we have two people of the same profession on every case. We have two nurses on records. We have two life planners on those cases. And we re-review a certain percentage of records, as part of our proprietary process to ensure quality. Clients need all information in a usable, shareable document. The amount of time, energy and money saved with shareable, usable document has a big impact.

How do you manage remote teams?

One of the challenges of having a remote workforce is fostering a sense of community. We struggled with this a few years ago. We have worked hard in last two years to bring people back together and make them feel part of a community. We learned that people who feel connected in a community collaborate better as a team. Each team member is an individual working remotely, but they have to come together to collaborate. Our team members are all across country and in Canada. So we instituted a number of things.

We used social media to our best advantage. We launched an internal social-media network to keep people connected. We have virtual meetings so we can see each other. We revamped our training process so we have online training modules interspersed with live modules.

We work off of an internal network called Ning. We wanted a private medium for our people. The social media is totally internal and creates a friendly virtual office environment. We went through rebranding recently, and our new brand is critical to creating a family. We want to make sure we're all on the same page with our vision and what we're about. We're really living and breathing what we're asking our clients to do. Ning is like an internal Facebook. It's fully branded. We even branded our teams, a More Team and a More membership. We have a Twitter feed, a blog, and chat rooms. Teams can discuss casework issues and ask and answer questions. There's an events section. People can upload photos and celebrate birthdays. It's very interactive.

Did this take a long time to set up?
No, it didn't take that long to put together. What took a long time was finding Ning, the vehicle that was going to satisfy our needs. A lot of the social-media networks become public. We wanted a private service. Our COO and marketing manager did all of this. We put this thing up, and about 90% of our people dove into it and have remained active. They were starved for a way to connect, to get to know each other, and to engage through an easy vehicle, and that made them feel a part of the family.

Where did the concept for Med Legal come from?
I founded Med Legal ten years ago. I'm a nurse by background. I went to nursing school in Madison, WI, but I'm a native Californian. Previously, I built and operated an outpatient surgery center, Outpatient Surgical Medical Unit, in Santa Monica, CA. It's still running. It was bought by orthopedic surgeons, and now it's called something else. During that time, I came across the field of legal-medical consulting. I had experience with surgery cases in the surgery center, and I spent a year researching the medical field. I realized there was a lot of opportunity. There had to be a better way for attorneys to work within the realm of bodily-injury cases. My theme is to work differently and smarter. The surgery center was ahead of the curve, but now there are 5,000 centers, and it's an $8 billion industry.

People are catching up to us now in the medical-records-review industry. Initially, I saw there would be a better way for attorneys and paralegals to work. Just because this is how they've always done it—attorneys and paralegals going through all the documents—that doesn't mean they should keep doing it. In bodily-injury cases, everything is in the medical records. Typically, the law brings experts into everything, except in this case: paralegals with no medical training review all these medical records. It didn't make good sense. So now we bridge the gap between the medical and legal worlds. We have people who are highly skilled professionals analyze medical records and bills and determine future care. Our clients are insurance carriers, law firms, self-insured companies, litigation-management companies, even the Department of Justice. Ten years after we started, this arena of medical-records analysis is still young. We've been singing this song for the past decade, but partly because of the economic crisis in 2008, people's ears are finally perking up.

In talking with insurance carriers and corporations, I've learned they have no idea what they're spending in medical-records review. There are no tracking measures, no metrics. So our proposition was to take this out from paralegals and attorneys and unbundle it to people who can do it better, faster, and cheaper. We can have an impact on the indemnity side and the liability side, in settling earlier and reducing damages. It's pretty exciting to be in this position. We're looking to stay at the forefront of this.

And to that end, you are now on the LEDES Committee?

That's right. I'm on the LEDES® [Legal Electronic Data Exchange Standard] Oversight Committee. The committee sets all legal billing codes for law firms to bill third parties. UTBMS Codes function as a common global language used to bill for services between law firms and third parties, like client corporations. For example, in our industry, insurance companies don't know what they spend on bodily-injury cases. Part of the problem is that there are no codes for medical review, medical-billing compilation, auditing, etc. And so, with no billing codes, they have no good way of tracking their spend in our arena. Law firms bill for generic hours for medical-record reviews, and insurance companies don't know who is doing what. We need to have codes in place so the law firms can bill appropriately and track their work according to codes and so the insurance companies can understand the amount of money they're spending in this area.

Will law firms appreciate these codes as well?
Absolutely. The truth is law firms don't appreciate who's doing what in their firm either. Without appropriate billing codes, they don't know how to focus on tasks with a higher value than medical-billing work. Typically, paralegals and associates are doing this kind of work anyway. They are the wrong people to be doing it, because it's not the highest billing use of their time.

So you were able to participate on the committee and develop new codes. What kinds of codes did you come up with?
We added one Activity code and three Expense codes. Every couple of years, the LEDES® Committee revises and updates the codes. So with my participation on the committee, I've been successful in getting codes established for expenses and activities related to our industry. I've been on the committee for over a year. The process to add new codes went on for two months and culminated on August 30. It will have a huge impact on the industry. And it will be profitable for everyone involved.

Do electronic medical records present any new issues?
E-records present some difficulty, because the new layout of these e-medical records requires professional expertise to decipher. I don't think there will be more of a need for our work. The format that all attorneys and paralegals are used to looking at is going to change, so that's going to change how they approach it now.

How do you define value?
It all goes back to empowering people to work more productively. Our value is in our level of analysis. We can extract information from medical records and bills and put them in easy-to-read text. We understand our client's needs. We can identify and articulate the risks and opportunities. Our expertise is what allows us to have a growing business and not become a commodity. We're always looking ahead and using technical resources to further enhance the analysis in our reports. We customize. We do large-scale

cases, and we maintain constant vigilance and cooperation such that we can change our approach midstream if we have to. With our unbundled, best-in-class team approach, we have an incredible level of flexibility and responsiveness to our clients.

What advice would you give to law grads?

I think there's still a ton of opportunities. I'm still excited and optimistic about everything that's going on. People are coming out of law school today with a great education and skill set, but working in a law firm will be tough. This whole industry is changing at such a speed that I think people will have to be creative.

Are there specific educational tracks for people who want to work in your field?

Absolutely. A number of schools and private companies are training experienced nurses how to analyze records in complex litigation. There are numerous schools offering life-care planning with clinical experience. So there are advanced degrees in education in all three of our service lines. There are also nurse paralegal programs. There is sort of a debate within our profession about nurse paralegals. The basic issue is that a nurse already went to school on a specialized path that requires more schooling than becoming a paralegal. So rather than a nurse becoming a paralegal, a nurse interested in more schooling could instead become a certified legal nurse consultant. In our case, I can see building out our teams, and we sort of played with these roles, including looking for roles for attorneys in our team. We love the paralegal world that we have. The paralegal editor role is critical in keeping our analyses robust. We've even brought pharmacists into a team. There are all kinds of professions in our legal world. We're creating new roles for people with a variety of different experiences.

What's on the horizon for MedLegal as a business?

Over the last two years, we've been looking for an opportunity to form a partnership. We had been looking for investors to realize our vision for MedLegal, and we realize we need other resources—talent, money, and technology—to take us to the next level. We are merging MedLegal with a company in our space, a global litigation-service provider called Elevate. The merger will result in the improvement of our technology resources, and that will impact the delivery of our reporting and turnaround time. We'll be able to address pricing and other aspects. We'll be able to compete in the insurance world, take on much larger-scale project work, and enhance our value to our clients.

Mitt Regan

Professor of Law
Georgetown University Law Center
Washington, DC

"The recession has put in-house counsel in the driver's seat. They can dictate to firms now. Things are not going to go back to the way they were before the recession. I think that the changes are permanent."

What drove you to write *Eat What You Kill: The Fall of a Wall Street Lawyer*?
I read an article in *The National Law Journal* about a partner sentenced to federal prison for not disclosing a conflict of interest in a corporate bankruptcy case. I saw his photo. He looked like an average guy. And I started talking to the people involved. At the same time, I read several thousand documents relating to his trial, the bankruptcy, and financing transactions in which the company in bankruptcy had been involved. Eventually, I used the case as a vehicle to discuss changes in the profession that began in the '70s and '80s, when relationships between clients and law firms were dissolving, from long-term to short-term. The sources of those changes are the same as the changes happening in the last several

years. There is more pressure on in-house counsel, which reflects the larger impact of increasing demands on them from their client companies. And so I explored the ways those relationships had changed. Firms in the legal-services market have become competitive, more entrepreneurial, and more aggressive. These trends are creating new pressures for partners in established law firms.

Where do you think the legal industry is today?
The period I discussed in my book was from 1980 to around 2004, which was the year the book was published. The sense then was that, "Boy, things have gotten competitive." A common complaint was that corporate clients weren't loyal, but at the same time, when firms got business, they were still in the driver's seat. Competition hadn't fully taken hold. In the early 2000s before the 2008 crash, clients pushed back. Corporate in-house departments grew and added more sophisticated people, and companies pressured their legal departments to cut the costs of legal services, which were spiraling. Hildebrandt says law-firm rates increased from 2001 to 2007 an average of 6% to 8% a year, with most pricing done by hourly billing.

There were two stages that happened before 2008. First, around 1980, the long-term client/firm relationships started breaking apart. Clients shopped around, and lawyers moved among firms. So firms competed for both clients and firms. This was a market revolution. Second, in the mid-2000s, clients increased pressure on firms for more efficiency. This is sparking an efficiency revolution: a major shift in how services are being organized and delivered. These trends were in place before the downturn.

Over time, maybe ten years, given the conservative culture of the profession, the trends would eventually have had an impact. But with the downturn, the firms were caught with excess capacity, and the demand from companies dropped. Corporate clients remain under serious pressure to do more with less, and in-house attorneys are being asked to justify legal spending in terms of outcomes. So client companies are pressuring legal departments to structure work so that outside law firms share some of the risk. If litigation doesn't turn out well, the firms earn less. Budgets create incentives for efficiency, not just for billing more hours. There are now more efforts to devise metrics to measure the performance of firms, from collaboration to billing to labor, and so on. This is the efficiency revolution.

Some firms are waiting for things to go back to where they were before the recession.

The recession has put in-house counsel in the driver's seat. They can dictate to firms now. Things are not going to go back to the way they were before the recession. I think that the changes are permanent.

How do you define value?

The ACC has the Value Challenge. They've been sponsoring various discussion sessions around the country between general counsel and law firms. In some areas, like certain litigation that's reasonably regular and predictable, you can develop parameters, based on past data, for the projected value of a claim or a body of legal work. There are case-assessment tools that estimate the likelihood of resolution, the time it might take, the cost of trial versus settlement, and so on.

Transactions are more difficult. General counsel are building and relying on preferred provider networks to use a limited number of firms, basing certain things on metrics, but they're also encouraging people in the business units to work more closely and earlier with lawyers. There are also performance metrics and surveys and different ways to track and provide objective and subjective information about law firms and individual lawyers.

Is the impact of business pressure changing the role of what a lawyer does?

One ongoing concern is that, when we get out of the recession, there is going to be less need for lawyers and, therefore, less need for law graduates. With efficiency comes a delegation of work, including moving legal work that can be automated and done by software, away from lawyers. Alternative service providers are doing more than document review and legal research.

The challenge, especially in legal education, is figuring out what positions might be out there in several years that don't fit the conventional role of lawyer. New jobs will require different skills and different sets of knowledge in law and technology. These roles will provide value to clients, but they won't necessarily be roles that people who romanticize traditional law practice will recognize.

Would you go to law school today?

I would go if I had a pretty good idea of what I wanted to do, had a realistic sense of how to make that happen, and didn't expect to become fabulously wealthy from law practice. The debt alone today makes it a different kind of decision. Applications are down this year across the country.

What are law schools doing today to adapt to this changing marketplace?

The first thing law schools are trying to do is to get a sense of what's been going on. They're asking questions. "Is this a cyclical thing, a phase in a business cycle? Will things reset, or does this represent a major shift?" We think it represents a more significant shift. So we want a sense of what parts of the market are affected the most.

National law schools have sent a large percentage of their students to large law firms. That number has declined in the last couple years. We're trying to think through what can make students competitive in traditional markets but also competitive in emerging, non-traditional markets. The message we're getting from practitioners is we need to do more to give students a concrete sense of how law is practiced today.

Firms inevitably have to train new lawyers. You learn by working with lawyers. In law school, there has not been a lot of work done in teams and not a lot of training in open-ended problem-solving. We've not often had occasion for students to grapple with messy situations. So our stance is that, to prepare students for this emerging world, we need to make law school more meaningful for practice. We're not talking about narrow rote skills; we're talking about complex cognitive competencies that go beyond traditional legal reasoning.

Does that mean starting some kind of apprenticeship system in law school?

Apprenticeship, historically, is what associates experienced early in their careers at law firms. Clients, in the past, had been willing to pay for this training, so it worked. Now, with clients in the driver's seat, they don't want to pay to train first- or second-year associates. They don't want to fund their apprenticeship and subsidize their training, especially with high associate turnover. So firms are turning to law schools for help, but law schools can't take this on by themselves. We're a different environment. We can't replicate a firm environment, but we can do more than we have done. The clinical programs at Georgetown are ranked #1 in the country. But we're also looking to incorporate experiential facets in our non-clinical courses.

It seems like a bind for law schools. They're being pressured to train students for firms that may or may not hire them or can't afford to hire them.

There are certainly pressures everywhere in small and large firms, and they're all looking to hire graduates who can hit the ground running. We train our students in broader cognitive skills so they can function in a variety of practice settings. We're expanding education to train students in the kinds of capabilities beyond what we've done, those capabilities that lawyers can use in variety of settings.

What kinds of capabilities are you trying to develop in students?

One trend that seems to be clear is there is an increase in the number of firms that represent business clients and a corresponding decrease in those firms that represent individuals. Because of technology today, you can work solo and do sophisticated corporate work. We're looking seriously at developing business and financial literacy in our students. We want them to be able to act more as an adviser who works with people to resolve or prevent problems rather than give strict legal advice. Good lawyers can play the adviser role. They will have to gain much of that experience over time, but we can begin in law school to start seeing the world through the client's eyes. More broadly, lawyers who work in all sectors will need to engage in complex problem-solving, develop the capacity for providing advice to clients that takes account of both legal and non-legal considerations, build and work effectively in teams, and know how to communicate with multiple audiences. The best lawyers do this, but they traditionally haven't learned it in law school. That needs to change.

Josh Linkner

CEO and Managing Partner
Detroit Venture Partners, LLC
Detroit, MI

"Value has to do with results. I could accomplish a huge amount in fifteen minutes. You could spend ten hours doing nothing. So who created more value? It's about impact, not hours."

How did you get interested in entrepreneurialism?

I started my first company when I was twenty. It was a computer company. I would build computers out of my college apartment and sell them. In 1995, I launched a company doing web design. No one had heard of the internet, so we had fun shaking things up. I loved improving the nature of the business world.

How did you start writing your book?

I became obsessed with creativity and how creativity has become the currency of success. I became interested in creativity as a concept. I did research and conducted interviews. My book *Disciplined Dreaming* launched February 2011. It took a few years to write. Now I teach an undergraduate course from the book. It's nice to make a difference. I'm an adjunct professor. I teach on the Dearborn campus of the University of Michigan.

Why did you choose Detroit to start your firm?

We're all from Detroit, and four partners are from Lansing. I'm from Detroit. I'm a hometown guy. I have a lot of history here. My grandparents are from here. I felt like Detroit was ideal for a venture-capital firm to invest in start-ups.

What did you do before Detroit Venture Partners?

DVP is my fifth company. I started four of the five in Detroit. I was the CEO of ePrize for eleven years. We had 450 people working there and $100 million in annual revenue.

What is DVP doing in Detroit?

We're investing in technology start-ups in Detroit to rebuild entrepreneurial fire and passion. Our investment firm follows an all-digital strategy. We invest in start-ups working in the online, digital realm.

Are there parallels today between business and the law?

Creativity is the key to success in both law and business. Today, most industries are about interpretation and applying creativity, whether creating a new service or advocating for a client.

What kinds of new operating models are you seeing?

37signals in Chicago has four employees with others all over the world, with totally weird hours. There are flat organizations in which nobody has a title. Organizations are being built around deploying creativity rather than just following the rules.

What Detroit companies have you invested in?

We've made some cool investments here in Detroit. We backed a company called Are You A Human, which replaces CAPTCHA with a game. (CAPTCHA refers to those wavy letters you type in for online authentication.) They solved a problem in a creative way. They made a game out of it, secured funding, and are building a business around that. Today, you can't win with just good customer service. That's a given. Otherwise, you're out of business. Today, you have to solve problems in unique and compelling ways. You have to apply creativity liberally.

We also invested in Gumshoe. Gumshoe fuses the digital and physical worlds in a mystery game, using real-world and digital assets. I think to me what that symbolizes is people are imagining things differently. I invite my team to ask the three magic questions: "Why," "What if," and "Why not?" Those questions force you to challenge conventional wisdom.

What's your advice to large firms that are slow to change or, really, any lawyer who has to overcome years of habitual thinking?

There are a few ways to do it. It's all about fresh thinking. The people who get crushed in negotiation or in court, they come out and say, "Yeah, but it's the way we've always done it." The people who take creative angles will come out ahead. Whether the organization is big or small, old or new, it's imperative to think like a start-up. Big firms tend to protect old ideas. Today, you need new ones. The problem is lawyers flock and find safety in numbers. Once they see a flock, the lawyers of the future should sprint in the opposite direction. People spend so much time playing it safe, but today playing it safe has become the riskiest move of all.

People in an existing organization don't just spontaneously start to think creatively. It takes education. Everyone has to understand and be on the same page. Do you spend any time educating organizations in this way?

I spend a lot of time educating, actually. I do a lot of speaking. I'm brought into associations and organizations, and I try to get them to think differently. I really believe this is an imperative. Since 2008, the world has changed, and we can no longer rely on the models of the past and hope to win. The world is very different. Change arrives with dizzying speed and increasing complexity. Last year's game plan is the way to mediocrity or death. We have to change the way we do business. It's not just about products or websites. It's about everything, including the practice of law.

Lawyers tend to think of what can go wrong, while entrepreneurs try to find a way to make things go right. Is that fair to say?

To me, the world doesn't need more people pointing fingers and telling you all the reasons things can't work. Blaming doesn't add value. You either add value or deplete it. You're contributing, or you're a parasite. Lawyers get a bad rep from telling you why things can't work. That's not adding value. I like this old Chinese proverb: "The man who said it can't be done should not interrupt the men doing it."

Lawyers are now exploring ways to dismantle the billable hour and find other ways to measure value. How do you talk about value?

The billable hour is a ridiculous way to define value. It's archaic and silly. In an hour, two people could accomplish radically different things. Value has to do with results. I could accomplish a huge amount in fifteen minutes. You could spend ten hours doing nothing. So who created more value? It's about impact, not hours.

How do you create the opportunity for creativity in a company or firm?

I talk to companies about the 5% strategy. If you take 5% out of a forty-hour work week, that's just two hours a week. Spend those two hours in collaboration, ideation, or go to a local art museum. Be head's up rather than head's down. Lawyers are typically head's down in their documents. When you're head's up, you notice things. My advice to lawyers who want to make a difference for their clients is to spend more time being head's up.

Ellen Rosenthal

CHIEF COUNSEL, PFIZER LEGAL ALLIANCE
VP AND ASSISTANT GENERAL COUNSEL
PFIZER INC.
NEW YORK, NY

"The vision of the Legal Alliance is to reinstate the lawyer as trusted advisor whose value to the client develops through a long-term, secure partnership."

Did you do anything differently during the 2008–2009 financial crisis?

Amy Schulman, Pfizer General Counsel, launched the Pfizer Legal Alliance in March 2009. The Alliance was in part the realization of a vision that Amy had about the practice of law. Some of the restructuring of Pfizer's existing relationships with external counsel was no doubt facilitated by the change in the legal market as a result of the financial turmoil. This turbulence gave clients more bargaining power and likely facilitated the ability to restructure the relationships and launch the Alliance at that time. I joined Pfizer shortly after the Alliance had been launched and saw my job as introducing an infrastructure to enable the Alliance to become a long-term enterprise and to adapt smoothly as it matured.

What were you doing before you joined Pfizer?

I was in-house counsel at Mount Sinai Medical Center and Continuum Health Partners for a combined nine years prior to joining Pfizer. During the financial crisis, the healthcare world experienced huge pressure due to the rise of healthcare costs and the drop in reimbursements. Government tax-generated revenues and most hospital reimbursement is government funded.

Have you done anything differently since then (for example, in terms of hiring practices, relationships with firms, use of legal-process outsourcing)?

One of the hallmarks of the Alliance is its collaborative nature. It is a partnership between Pfizer and 19 law firms that each work on an annual flat fee rather than by the hour. The model is transforming the way legal services are delivered and valued. Together, Pfizer and the firms continually create and recreate cross-firm teams for projects based on expertise and experience. We have the best lawyers from across Alliance firms working on our projects—one might have experience with a product, another may be an expert in scientific evidence, and another could bring expertise in procedural issues affecting a case. It is really fantastic. We have brought together all of these lawyers who had not previously collaborated, and as a result Pfizer receives better legal counsel and, often, better outcomes.

We have introduced completely new approaches to developing young lawyers in the law firms and inside Pfizer. We have a "roundtable" comprised of top associates from the firms who are paired with Pfizer mentors for projects, such as running our CLE program, and they learn about the business in a more formal way. This year through our Junior Associate program, we hired three first-year lawyers who rotate for two years between Pfizer and an Alliance firm learning to compare the way in-house counsel and firm counsel approach a similar issue.

How do you manage educating everyone about the new methods?

My first task was to educate Pfizer's in-house lawyers about what the Alliance is and how it works. The information was disseminated throughout Pfizer among the ranks of lawyers, many of whom have daily interactions with law firms. It took some time to educate both Pfizer lawyers and firm lawyers beyond the leadership levels on how the Alliance worked and how to address the novel financial arrangements in working together.

I spent the first several months on the job visiting every practice group at Pfizer. I walked everyone through the nuts and bolts of the Alliance as well as sharing the overall vision for the Alliance. That made a huge difference in integrating the Alliance within the Legal Division. It is now part of our culture.

What was that overall vision for the PLA?

The vision of the Alliance is to reinstate the lawyer as trusted advisor whose value to the client develops through a long-term, secure partnership. A core tenet of the Alliance is about the value that kind of relationship brings to Pfizer and the satisfaction it provides to the lawyer. That is why we are committed to maintaining a stable group of firms within the Alliance to the extent that is possible. The firms are incentivized to know us better, because their work becomes more meaningful and, ultimately, more efficient as they learn more about us with each engagement. Alliance firm lawyers know the players and the background by participating in internal business and legal strategy meetings. Pfizer lawyers know the firm lawyers, and we can almost speak in shorthand. The idea is to develop Alliance firm counsel as an extension of our in-house staff.

In addition, to promote that vision, the Alliance takes a leap forward to build a truly innovative economic relationship between the lawyer and client. The Alliance financial relationship functions entirely without reference to the billable hour. We are building relationships by removing bad incentives and, instead, instituting incentives that reward the delivery of value through better, more efficient legal counsel and cross-firm knowledge sharing and collaboration.

How are the outside firms paid?

We have 19 firms in the Alliance, and all are paid an annual flat fee. In December of every year we set fees for the next year. There's no incentive for doing work for which you don't have the best lawyer. There is every incentive for firms to collaborate and use the best expertise in the right place and time.

The most surprising thing about the Alliance is that our lawyers have grown to know each other so well that Pfizer lawyers are not always leading the formation of cross-firm teams. The firm lawyers now know what lawyers at other firms are really good at, and because they have learned each other's strengths, they're able to build and rebuild teams for us using the best of the best.

Here's a good example of what the Alliance can accomplish. In an enormous mass tort case, we received an order to do several hundred depositions in a very short timeframe. We brought together 52 junior associates from Alliance firms. We called them the "associate army" and trained them in an associate "boot camp." They learned to take depositions and understand the medical issues, and then they were sent across the country to take the depositions. We were able to report back to the court that we had indeed succeeded in an otherwise nearly impossible assignment.

What size law firms do you use?

We use different firms for different purposes. We have representation from large global firms such as Skadden Arps and Clifford Chance, but more than half are smaller firms. We pair firms together. Sometimes we have bigger firms doing national strategy and smaller ones doing regional work. It depends on the needs for each legal matter.

Do you think this Legal Alliance is something that only a company like Pfizer can set up and run?

No, I don't think the Alliance approach is limited to Pfizer and I don't see any reason why the model is not scalable. We've built diversity initiatives, established an associate roundtable to develop junior-level talent, and done a lot of things that a company half our size wouldn't necessarily do. But as long as a company has a predictable legal spend it can accomplish goals similar to those that we have achieved.

Approximately 70 percent of Pfizer's global legal spend is handled within the flat-fee structure of the PLA. A smaller company would clearly not need as many law firms and could structure things differently. For example, they could set flat fees for predictable spending and reserve some budget for new large litigations which, for a smaller company, would significantly affect the equation. Maybe a company would need only three or five firms. From a financial perspective, being able to set the outside-counsel budget at the beginning of the year is an incredible thing. We know what we will spend on legal fees at the beginning of the year. Our finance department loves that.

Do you feel cost pressure from other parts of the company?

In any company, the legal division is always viewed as a cost center, and the pressure is to reduce costs. While cost-cutting was not the main purpose of setting up the Alliance, we've reduced legal spend and proven that every year. Our fee system rewards efficiency. For example, overstaffing a matter is against everyone's interest in a flat-fee model, as is preparation of a lengthy memo of law when all we need is a quick answer. We want our lawyers to pick up the phone proactively and tell us their view on risks associated with a certain activity without feeling that they will be perceived as drumming up new business.

What is the role of in-house counsel in managing outside work?

In-house counsel is getting much more sophisticated and involved in developing strategy with outside counsel. Our lawyers manage work, but we have removed bill review, which is essentially archeology, not management, as a component of oversight of outside counsel. In the absence of reviewing bills or talking in terms of hours, we have developed tools to facilitate communications with outside counsel. This ensures we're aligned on deliverables, timelines, and staffing at the start of new matters and through the life of ongoing matters. We focus on tasks and outcomes instead of hours and dollars in supervising the work.

Where does the drive for change come from, the firms or the clients?

In the case of the Pfizer Legal Alliance, the drive for change came from Pfizer. In my experience speaking with others working in this area, it most often seems to be the case that the client drives the change. General Counsel Amy Schulman came to Pfizer from one of our PLA firms. While she was on the firm side, what she enjoyed most was building relationships with clients—and she saw the billable hour as an impediment. She wanted to pick up the phone and alert a client to pay attention to a new legal issue, but would be concerned that quite possibly the reception could be, "You're looking for a way to grow your business," rather than "Thank you for looking out for my interests."

Amy had a vision, and she's very persuasive and charismatic and had a lot of credibility behind this vision because she was a successful lawyer in private practice. Law firms tend to be more traditional. Many PLA firms have been eager to learn how to change, and they truly enjoy being in the Alliance and learning how to be path breakers in this effort. But without Pfizer having led the charge, it wouldn't have happened.

You're really digging into how a particular law firm works.

We've taken the position that we have to work closely with our firms on every aspect of handling our matters. Many in-house counsel don't take this approach, but we have chosen to be more proactive in this way. Also, apart from managing the legal work from a substantive perspective, we are learning together with the firms how to be more efficient. We give firms permission to not write the proverbial memo or to assign junior lawyers. We work with them on how to streamline their work for us, and we're confident that this work is still of the highest quality.

Every firm in the Alliance has an assigned senior partner—a "relationship partner"—who serves as the main point of contact. We have a counterpart at Pfizer who manages the relationship with the law firm: a "PAL," Pfizer Alliance Leader. Because it would be impossible for me to oversee the work of 19 firms, the PALs and relationship partners review the firm portfolio of work together on a routine basis. They keep things on track, monitor new matters, and look at new opportunities for the firm, for Pfizer, and for the development of their attorneys. The PALs then report back to me. This has been a good way of managing the enormous workload across the globe. Because we do not yet have a new metric for value, when we sit down with firms and talk about whether they're doing too much or not enough work, we have to find our way together, and we depend on trust from both sides. When we have given a flat-fee budget and halfway through the year they tell us that they're spending ahead of the projected rate, we'll sit down and try to understand where and why that is happening and manage the work. In an extreme situation, we might move work to other firms, but generally we can prioritize and stage some work to lighten the workload.

How are you using new technology to help manage workload?

We've developed a monthly template that firms provide to us. It lists the top matters for the year and the month, identifies the level of effort being invested in the matter, the staffing, and any changes to the matter beyond the "baked in" assumptions. We have an intranet website for the PLA with designated practice-group areas. We also have a robust twice-yearly 360 process for evaluating the firms and the firms evaluating each other that is operated through the website to facilitate the gathering of feedback on the firms' performance from our lawyers across the globe.

So you're taking an informal process and putting it into a formal system?

To replace bills and time sheets as a management tool, we are trying to manage workload through close communication and jointly monitoring the work being performed and looking at outcomes. That is where the measurement of value has to go. We have to measure the value received by the client, as opposed to counting the hours invested by the provider.

How do your firms like the Alliance system?

It's a challenge to introduce anything that people haven't done before. To realize the financial incentives inherent in a flat fee, law firms have to challenge themselves to do things differently. This can sometimes be difficult at first, but our firms are now feeling like this is a normal way of doing business and understanding how to work in this model. We at Pfizer are doing better at working within this model, and we are running smoothly.

It takes a little while to get used to it. One challenge is integrating what we are doing into the larger firm communities to which the teams that work for Pfizer belong. It can be difficult for certain large firms, given their operational infrastructure, to incorporate a model that rejects the billable hour, which is built on a profitability model based on billable time. For example, many associates are promoted or given bonuses based on high numbers of annual hours, while our work rewards the firm when the associates work fewer hours. The firms' compensation model runs counter to our interests.

The lawyers who work on Pfizer matters greatly enjoy working for Pfizer because they love the work and because they enjoy working within the Alliance and benefitting from the camaraderie it has inspired. They're often working as colleagues with their past competitors.

What trends do you see in the next three to five years?

I think the movement toward streamlined, efficient legal counsel has traction this time. People have said this for a decade. Others are not necessarily doing what we're doing at Pfizer, but they are doing more work on alternative-fee bases and with fewer firms (in order to have deeper relationships with those fewer firms). I would love to see more companies adopt some of things we're doing to promote collaboration, knowledge-sharing, and community, and that may come as clients pursue convergence programs and alternative fees. I also foresee others hiring younger lawyers in-house and training them jointly with their firms to develop "home grown" in-house talent. I hope to see more of that in the next few years.

Michael Roster

Co-Chair, ACC Value Challenge
Steering Committee
Pasadena, CA

"Law firms fell for the mistaken notion that all they had to sell was hours, when, in fact, it is expertise that they have to sell, and expertise is a far more profitable concept for both sides if managed appropriately."

How has your thinking about value in legal services changed over the years?

I started practicing law in 1973 and spent the next 20 years—before I went in-house as Stanford's General Counsel—at what was originally the McKenna & Fitting firm and then with Morrison & Foerster. Until the mid- or late 1970s, virtually no law firm in the U.S.—or anywhere, for that matter—sent bills out based solely on hours. Many firms sent a bill with a single line, "for services rendered," while others included a narrative summary of the work that was done. In both instances, the amount was based on individual billing diaries, how efficient the billing partner felt he and others had been, and, most important, an estimate of the client's perceived value of the work. Many clients were on long-term, fixed-price retainer relationships with their law firms, and many firms functioned as the client's general counsel.

Those arrangements had both strengths and weaknesses, but with the advent of the computer to keep track of work in lieu of handwritten billing diaries, the newly emergent in-house counsel, most of whom came from law firms, started to insist on seeing the computer printouts and started to say that is what they would pay and only what they would pay. To them, the computer printout had precision, and they inadvertently equated that precision with value. Firms initially resisted sending the computer printouts, which obviously were based solely on hours, but eventually capitulated and, along with consultants who were happy to provide advice, made it both an art and science to manage everything by hours. And along the way, firms fell for the mistaken notion that all they had to sell was hours, when, in fact, it is expertise that they have to sell, and expertise is a far more profitable concept for both sides, if managed appropriately.

In the late 1980s, Carl Leonard, our then-chair of Morrison & Foerster, decided to try to get the firm off billable hours, or at least as much as possible. We and other firms had been on billable hours for only 15 years or so, and Carl saw it was undermining the firm's core culture. Among other things, it skewed incentives, and it also was a disadvantage to us when competing for work. For example, based on our expertise and the fact that we might be handling large numbers of similar matters for a wide range of clients, we could give a client an answer in fifteen minutes with very high certainty, whereas a firm with lower hourly rates but with less expertise and less investment in knowledge management might get the work based on lower hourly rates, even though they might spend hours or even days and still might not be very certain of the answer. So Carl appointed an ad hoc committee that I chaired, and within the first 18 months, we had a large number of projects on an alternative-fee basis—although, I should note, I hate the phrase *alternative fees* and believe the discussion, both then and now, needs to be about value-based relationships.

I moved in-house in mid-1993 and was chair of the Association of Corporate Counsel in 2001. Seven years after that, Fred Krebs, then ACC's president, and Susan Hackett, then ACC's general counsel, called me. This was before the financial meltdown. They were hearing the same thing from a lot of corporate counsel, and as we all joked, it was not the normal whining about law firms. In fact, for years GCs were saying, in our off-the-record discussions at ACC annual meetings and elsewhere, the problems were less about cost and more about the fact that the firms were spinning wheels more and more and increasingly delivering a work product that wasn't in tune with the corporate clients' real needs. The *Wall Street Journal* article about how billing rates were about to exceed $1,000 an hour became another precipitating event, with CEOs and other senior managers throughout the U.S. going to the GCs and saying, *Don't you dare use firms with this kind of cost*. Fred and Susan said the frustration was getting much worse, and it was time to do something. As we discussed the situation with a number of key in-house and law-firm leaders, including at four focus groups around the country, it became obvious that the issue was about value, and that led to the launch of the ACC Value Challenge.

We also noted at the time that we will have succeeded if, in a year or two, in-house and law-firm attorneys were talking about value, and it's mind-boggling how quickly that came about. Obviously, the economic meltdown helped a lot, but I think we would have achieved the intended focus on value even without the downturn.

That said, I also appreciate there is a lot still to be done. Some firms and some companies are far along. Many firms are at 40% or more of their work being on a value basis (and we don't count blended rates or discounts as alternative fees). There are a number of major nationwide and even worldwide companies where 50% and even 80% or more of their legal work is now being done on a fixed price or other value-based arrangement. But many are still functioning in a very traditional—and very expensive—manner.

The profession is on a good trajectory to better define and deliver value, but I think it's important to recognize that we are also in a period of chaos, in a scientific sense. There are lots of natural phenomena and human phenomena where things go for a long time on a predictable, straight-line path and then suddenly go into what appears only as chaos. In the past three decades, we've learned a lot about these phenomena, including the incredible fact that most so-called chaotic periods share common characteristics (look up fractals and chaos if you would like to explore this further). So I tell both in-house and law-firm lawyers not to be surprised if people say one thing and do something else, or if things seem chaotic. Because I also note that most general counsel, and most law-firm managing partners, are happy to keep things in a steady state. Why make a major change if you don't need to, especially given how difficult it is to cope with what we all do day by day? But there inevitably will come what I call the moment of truth, client by client and firm by firm, where the status quo is no longer working. In a scientific sense, this is a time when things are no longer linear and instead appear chaotic and complex. And that's when you better be ready to manage change, and to do so decisively and with experience already under your belt as to what to do.

How difficult is it for law firms to move toward a model based on value?

Every law firm (or practice group or whatever) that changes its model says the same thing: the first year is awful. No matter how you plan for it, instituting these changes will be difficult, even if the participants think they are ready. On top of that, lawyers hate change, and they are very good at arguing why things won't work. They've been rewarded all through law school, on bar exams and in their early years of practice, for identifying as many nit-picky issues as possible and then talking endlessly about those issues, usually without then asking the important question whether or not the issues matter. So it's dreadful to get lawyers to change.

But once you get through it, virtually everyone finds it was worth it. Client costs will come down. Pricing will be largely fixed or contingent and with high predictability, and firms will be equally if not more profitable. Firms will also be much happier places to work, with far less turnover and with junior lawyers on the front line much sooner and with much greater professional satisfaction. The task for a law firm's chair will be to hold the place together during the transition, and firms that have been through the process know that it is a particularly difficult task to run the firm partly on hours and partly on a fixed-price system where profitability and attorney productivity need to be measured on a totally different basis. In fact, experience demonstrates that those who simply measure things during the transition based on shadow hours will find they are working against themselves and ultimately will fail.

Both Pfizer and Levi's are far along in their transformation. A number of other Fortune 50 companies are likewise far along in blowing up old arrangements. There's one company that reportedly moved all of its U.S. litigation in the past two years from 700 firms to 30 and in the process has over 80% of its U.S. litigation (both bet-the-company litigation and routine, recurring litigation) now on a fixed-price arrangement, with a reduction in cost of 25% to 50%, better outcomes, and strong profitability for the participating law firms.

Companies making the change have also concluded that success requires re-establishing longer-term trusted relationships with firms and devising fixed-price portfolios or similar arrangements, and they likewise avoid hourly-based incentive systems that create pointless work. Jeffrey Carr, the GC of FMC Technologies in Houston, has created an incentive arrangement that rewards not just quantifiable results but also qualitative performance, such as communication, access, etc. The overall message in Jeff's system and similar systems is that you have to solidify mutual understandings with your law-firm vendors. You learn how to set the price and track quality and results, and once you do that, you no longer waste internal resources with micromanaging.

How do you get the ball rolling for moving work to fixed-price portfolios?

Law is remarkably predictable, even though lawyers say it's not. You can look at what's gone on for the past two to three years at a given client, and when you have that data (and close enough is good enough for these purposes), you find you actually can predict legal costs going forward. You see what the client spent in the past, for example, on all of its labor or environmental work, and you can commit to doing it for 10% to 25% less than that amount. It's not a discounted hourly rate but a fixed-cost reduction. And as long as you are managing the process and the effective deployment of expertise and resources, you quickly find you can do the work for this lesser amount and still achieve improved outcomes and actually increased profitability at the firm. And that's why my task is also to get general counsel to understand that, if a firm has reduced your cost 25% and is providing high predictability and better outcomes, you should be delighted that the firm is as profitable as or even more profitable than before. That's how we run our companies: reduce cost of production, improve quality, and increase profitability. So why should we begrudge a law-firm vendor that is similarly incentivized on our behalf?

You will find a similar pattern for individual cases. For example, a lot of our litigation at Stanford was workforce-related. When I was GC, we looked at the numbers, and it turned out that every case was costing us about the same amount to litigate, and virtually every settlement was within the same range. The only reason people didn't think it was predictable was because no one had looked! The firms have data, but they've never looked at it. Same for clients. And then those who start looking at data often get sidetracked on minutiae. For example, no one can remember hundreds of task codes, and requiring every billing entry to be laboriously coded only adds cost with little if any benefit. Rather, you can look at past matters and get a rough estimate of what it costs to do a simple deposition versus a difficult one. You'll find a fairly predictable pattern on these and similar tasks so you know what each element might cost going forward, and with that fairly basic information, you can develop a pretty accurate estimate of cost for virtually every matter and for specific tasks. Even better, in my mind, is to take on a whole portfolio and to do so for a fixed-price, because now you are managing a wide range of work and can make rational decisions about the best place to devote resources in order to achieve the best outcomes.

We build hundred-story skyscrapers at fixed prices, so why can't lawyers do their work with similar predictability? And we clients find it especially ironic that the typical sales pitch made to us by a law firm is that the firm has handled hundreds of similar matters and has the best lawyers in the country or even the world for these matters, but when we ask what it will cost, the answer typically is that the firms have no idea. Another analogy I like to make is: imagine if you built a house by the hour. Do you think your architect, general contractor, subcontractors, and others would control costs? Or be efficient? Nope. Even with the uncertainties of building a house, or even a hundred-story skyscraper, those professionals have learned how to fix or at least estimate cost. We lawyers need to step up to the plate and do the same.

One final point. Every few months I get a call from a GC who is in the middle of making the change or has completed it, and every call is largely the same: "Now that I've looked at the numbers, the patterns are unmistakable. Now that we've made the change, our legal costs are down 25%." It's almost always this number. And: "Why didn't we do this sooner?"

How else, beyond fixed pricing, can you measure value in the relationship between client and outside counsel?
I was at a conference two years ago. One panelist was from a Midwest firm that was pushed by a client to do a fixed-price portfolio of litigation. The first few months, he said, were a disaster, because firm management thought the only way to break even, or at least not lose too much, would be to use the lowest-cost lawyers possible. But the firm quickly started to see that was a totally wrong concept, and that the most cost-effective way to handle the work would come by staffing the matters with people who had the highest skills and expertise for a given task, not who was cheapest. Toward the end of the first year, the numbers were working very nicely. Also, associates who previously had avoided these matters because they couldn't rack up high hours now were very desirous of working on them since the associates were coming up the learning curve fast and were functioning as real front-line lawyers.

The long and short of it is, the firm got very good at handling the work. But then the responsible partner was asked to have lunch with the client's senior management, and he thought now they're going to put the squeeze on us and try to reduce the price. But it turns out the GC and other senior officers of the client used the lunch instead to thank the partner and the firm, with no intention of squeezing on cost. Rather, they said they were delighted with the predictability and reduced cost for the portfolio. But far more important, the company's bond rating had gone up, and its insurance premiums had gone down, largely as a result of the good litigation outcomes combined with a significantly reduced risk profile. This represented real value to the client.

The responsible partner who was describing this at the conference said, "It never crossed my mind our better management of the legal work would have had these very significant cost benefits to the client. In fact, the legal savings were modest compared to these other benefits, and in retrospect, this might have been a far more profitable way for the firm to measure value."

It's unlikely you can get a client to share these kinds of cost benefits (that is, millions of dollars in savings from bond offerings and insurance premiums), but even if it's not part of the fee itself, most CEOs and others will readily see the kind of value that is being brought to the company by law firms that function in this manner and will be far less concerned about legal costs, especially if the costs are predictable and the outcomes are measurably improved.

I think another important question is, "Why aren't law-firm attorneys regularly at the client's place of business?" A useful practice is to set up weekly or monthly on-site sessions to talk with the in-house lawyers and, more important, the relevant internal clients. For example, if you're handling HR work, you and the head of HR can cover a lot of items at once and in person, including current litigation and compliance matters, as well as looking at early warning signs, allowing the attorneys to take action before a reasonably simple item becomes a major problem. This also allows outside counsel to keep up with what's going on in the organization, with significant rewards to all sides. We saw this regularly at Stanford. The more a law firm could keep us out of trouble, the more valuable they were. And when the law-firm attorneys were working with us as if they were in-house, they could do their work with high efficiency and effectiveness. And for things like compliance, the attorneys were no longer sitting in a room and giving a boring lecture on preventative law; that usually wasn't preventing anything. Rather, they got very adept at knowing where the problems would likely arise and then started to think, "How do we reduce having those problems or, when they arise, handle them early on?" And managers knew they could call a lawyer without worrying about being billed, because the portfolios were at a fixed price.

Our legal costs at Stanford came down 25% with the firm attorneys being able to use offices on-site on a regular basis, schedule their own meetings with clients, and apply their skills as they thought appropriate. We also had, at Stanford, a non-lawyer Director of Legal Services who had prior management experience at several major law firms. Four or five years into the project, she came to me and showed me that we were running at half the litigation we had had in the past decade. So not only were costs down, but people weren't being tied up as much in depositions and other parts of litigation, there was much better and ongoing communication between the various units of the University and the Medical Center with counsel, and we had less reputational exposure that comes with litigation and other disputes. These are other ways that value can be provided.

How does anyone know how to change operating models? Do they hire consultants?

You have to learn by doing. You can hire consultants, and many have some very good tools, but you don't really understand the problems and the solutions until you commit to the change and then do it. Increasingly I can see benefits where an intermediary helps both sides work through the transition—to act somewhat as Switzerland in the process, a neutral party. Whoever plays that neutral role ideally will have been through the process before so they can recognize warning signs and provide solutions.

During the first year, the firms will often keep comparing everything with billable hours, including measuring whether or not the project is a success. But that approach guarantees a lose-lose result. Either the work comes in at more than would have been the case if it had been billed solely by hours, in which case the firm thinks it's a bad deal for the firm, or the work comes in at less than would have been the case with hours, in which case the client feels it has been screwed. More important, this use of shadow hours is a barrier to either side rethinking what they are doing, why they are doing it, and how they could do it better. If the firm instead focuses on overall profitability and results, everything else will quickly fall into place. The risk likewise is that the GC and other in-house lawyers will just keep asking for hours and likewise not rethink what they are doing. You need to get both the GCs and the firms to change their thinking in fundamental ways. It's a partnership, and both sides have to reengineer the entire process, with the goal of accomplishing at least one target and eventually all three:

(1) reduce total legal cost (in-house and law firm combined) by 25%;

(2) provide near certainty in cost; and/or

(3) significantly improve outcomes.

Both sides have to change, but firms have to confront very fundamental issues, like the whole associate structure, don't they?

This is one of the things firms eventually realize as they change their focus from hours to outcomes, efficiency, and predictability: they have to get away from leverage and high associate turnover. With fixed-price billing, high leverage destroys you. You can't put 30 people on a matter, and you realize you actually don't need 30 people and never did. Rather, you find the three or five who really know how to handle the matter. A lot of us think firms will get back to a two-to-one leverage (that is, two associates per partner) or even less. Some of the most successful firms actually have more partners than associates. It's also goofy to keep delaying the time we make a junior attorney a partner, other than to manipulate the average profit-per-partner numbers for various publications. Firms eventually learn that it makes much more sense to make highly capable lawyers a partner after five or six years. We know who has the skills by then, and this provides a commitment from everyone involved.

In almost every major firm in the country, 85% of associates are gone by the end of the sixth year. At least until the meltdown, the all-in cost per recruit was $250,000 to $400,000 just to get that recruit in the door. This includes sending people to law schools to interview, having the candidates interview for a day or two at the firm, and running the summer program, but it does not include what happens after they start work fulltime, including training. No other business runs itself this way. If you were using titanium and found that 85% was on the shop floor to be thrown out each day, you'd go out of business. Firms have been able to promote this kind of wasteful turnover because clients have been willing to pay for it, and clients have paid for it because they didn't understand the extraordinary (and unnecessary) costs of leverage and turnover.

Most firms will likely collapse under their own weight if they can't change the imbalance in the partner/associate model. Also, moving lawyers into the partnership sooner allows giving the key parts of the workforce a basic guaranteed income, with the rest being profit-sharing, and thus allows much more flexibility in the cost structure, including early warning signs if the firm isn't functioning efficiently. This is how client companies operate. It's only the law firms that somehow think they are comparable to a major business, but where they only expect an upside to the business, versus the reality of every other business where the value of stock and stock options can fluctuate widely and bonuses likewise can and will fluctuate widely.

Do we need law firms at all today, or are we moving toward completely new arrangements?

I know that various components of legal work can be unbundled, and that may be a useful model, for example, for certain types of legal research or document reviews. But law firms are an extraordinary type of knowledge-based enterprise, and shame on all of us for messing them up so terribly in the last several decades. We have some of the most talented people anywhere working at law firms. The reality is that for the tough matters you need smart people brainstorming with one another. I don't need lawyers to be robots; if that's what is involved in parts of legal work, there are a lot of other providers who can do the task. I need lawyers to make important breakthroughs, both large and small.

I also question the idea that lawyers can just work at home and that the firm of the future will be a virtual firm. At my prior law firms, what I call the lone wolves were always the most dangerous. These are the attorneys who insisted on working alone. They seldom if ever would check with others about what they might be missing or what other approaches might be considered. That's not good, because you don't get the best quality work that way, and unfortunately, unbundling functions and using virtual law firms often builds on the lone-wolf syndrome. To be creative and to find the risks and the breakthroughs, you need the interaction of highly skilled professionals. That's where a well-constituted law firm adds immense value. A strong firm culture greatly enhances its expertise through this process. The idea of work being unbundled and then handled by some robotic process can provide efficiencies, but there's always the risk that someone isn't seeing a pattern of facts or places where there are major vulnerabilities, because those processes are no longer part of the larger picture until they blow up in your face.

That isn't to say there aren't some very good, innovative approaches. For example, I had a major piece of litigation in the San Francisco Bay Area, and I found what amounts to a virtual law firm with three to four partners. They created a boutique and are still getting big company work, with very high praise from GCs. When they get a big matter, the permanent partners contact people they know, including very capable seasoned lawyers who are retired or doing other things, and from these people they assemble an extraordinary litigation team. The team members don't have to be in the same location or even close by. They often work together by phone, fax and computer, but they still got together periodically for face-to-face brainstorming sessions covering everything, and the team remains in place through the life of the litigation and then disbands.

Virtual teams are common now in other industries, but there are studies supporting the benefits of random interactions with diverse people. How can you recreate that with virtual teams?

There is something critical about being face to face and watching body language and getting to know your colleagues. Lawyers in my practice group at Morrison & Foerster were in at least six different cities, and I tried to make everyone, especially junior and mid-level associates, work for at least a week in another city. Having worked face to face with others in another geographic location, even for just a week, creates the foundation for a strong professional relationship and allows subsequent digital communication to go much more smoothly. Likewise, when I maintained offices in both LA and DC, the most important meetings were typically when someone drifted into my office on the third or fourth day and said, "I didn't want to bother you, but..." What ensued would often turn out to be the most important interaction during my time at the other office. But there would be barriers for someone to call me about it or to take my time during my first day or two. It's that regular presence that leads to these types of interactions. I don't discount that, with video conferencing, being physically present may be less important. But even then, periodic time to be together can be very beneficial.

What is the role of a servicing partner?

When I was in private practice, I never heard the term *servicing partner*, but a few years after being a general counsel, a number of us started to hear the term. As GCs, we love these so-called servicing partners because they answer our questions. And yet we found out the firms were firing them or at least de-equitizing them, because they were holding down average profits per partner—that is, the servicing partners were "only" making $600,000 a year and often had just one or two highly competent associates working with them. So while law-firm chairs didn't like servicing partners, we GCs loved them, because they give us and our clients what we need and want.

When you switch to fixed-price matters and portfolios, ironically the servicing partners and the people working with them become among the most profitable attorneys in the firm. They are highly responsive to clients. They answer tons of questions a day, and if they don't immediately know the answer, they say they want to check something and will get back to us later in the day, and they always do. GCs know these people by name, especially when we bring them questions for which the CEO or CFO wants an immediate answer or at least a ballpark answer. The servicing partners make GCs look good, and that's worth gold to a GC.

But even more to the point, on larger and ongoing matters, servicing partners and the people working with them produce highly valuable work product with minimal cost of production—the very components that make the work highly profitable once you're no longer measuring value by hours.

You mentioned legacy models in other industries that stick with tradition and eventually fail. Should law graduates be reviewing the operating models of potential employers to make sure these employers aren't about to go out of business?

If you had told people in the '70s that three of our major airlines—Pan Am, TWA, and Eastern—weren't just going to lose market share, but all three would soon be out of business, those people would've said you were crazy. The problem for those airlines was, "Why change something that's successful?" So senior management missed the changes taking place, and even if they had seen them, the legacy systems (computers, methods of servicing the aircraft, how one prices various routes) and everything else in the company would have worked against making change.

In the '80s, the Oldsmobile Cutlass was the best-selling sedan. Within a few short years, it didn't just lose market share; it disappeared. There are similar stories in retailing (A&P, Wards, and Circuit City versus Amazon, Target, and Walmart), publishing (magazines and newspapers everywhere), and computers and mobile phones (Alta Vista, Yahoo, and BlackBerry versus Google, Apple, and Android-based smartphones). Kodak invented digital photography, but everything in the company worked against using it, and the company instead remained focused on what worked well in the past: traditional film and the services that came with it.

When I was GC at Stanford, I wanted someone to live in my house in Southern California so it wouldn't be left empty, and since the federal Ninth Circuit courthouse is at the bottom of my hill, each year a clerk from the court would stay at the house. One of the clerks turned down offers from major firms everywhere and instead went to Bartlit Beck, a firm I hadn't heard of at the time.

This is a firm that has virtually never billed by the hour. They created this model to run their shop differently. It's based on value, and the firm has always been this way since its founding less than 20 years ago. The last I've looked, they have six partners per associate. They take the toughest litigation in the country and win it. Fred Bartlit wants real lawyers. I have visited the offices several times when I'm in Chicago, and they are constantly brainstorming about issues. They do a minimum of memo writing. They are constantly interacting with one another. They try mock cases in a

100-year-old courtroom that is at the core of their offices. In my friend's case, in his first year at the firm, he was running a big global case against a major New York firm, and he said they were going to beat the other side, and they did.

I appreciate that some people say the firm takes only bet-the-company cases and hires Supreme Court clerks and other very high-level lawyers, so it's not a model that can be replicated. To that, I say, "Nonsense." Any well-designed firm, including a small boutique, can follow this model and do extremely well, for both itself and its clients.

Can recent graduates find firms like this? First, given the job situation, recent graduates should take any decent job they can find. That said, they should at least be looking at firms where they will progress rapidly in the expertise they develop and the frontline work they are allowed to do. And they will find that the most rewarding professional careers will be at firms that have very low leverage and turnover and that are quickly migrating to value-based relationships with clients.

What might law schools do quickly to adapt to changes in the legal industry?

I think law schools need to teach their students how to be first-rate practicing lawyers. That means understanding substantive law. To achieve that goal, the case method is fine for a few weeks; it teaches a method of thinking. It makes no sense for three years. Most substantive law can be taught in a matter of days, and we do that with the bar courses quite successfully. But once a student learns how to think like a lawyer and then has mastered basic substantive law, the real task remains: teaching judgment and what I call *professional calibration*.

Some law schools are pushing interdisciplinary studies. That's okay for one or two courses, but at the end of the day, I don't care if you know business or engineering when as a GC I'm looking for good lawyers. I need to know that you can practice law.

For the past two years, I've been teaching an advanced contracts course at the University of Southern California. Most of the students are in their last semester of their third year. They all took contracts in their first year and then courses in real estate, corporations, etc. And yet, as is the case for most of the major law schools throughout the country, most of the students have never seen a contract while in law school. Law students throughout the U.S. are still taught by heavy reliance on appellate cases, something most practicing lawyers seldom if ever look at. The students largely have no idea what lawyers actually do, notwithstanding that legal practice is an extremely challenging, intellectual process. And the reason for this is that most of the tenured faculty have never practiced law or did so for only a few years. Imagine if we taught doctors this way: that is, with the students never seeing a patient and with teachers who don't know how to practice medicine or only did so for a year or two.

So I have the students in my class work with real contracts: Meg Whitman's employment agreement, Google's terms of use, law-firm-engagement letters, litigation-settlement agreements, etc. The students have to learn how to interpret and write a wide range of contracts. In the last third of the course, the students work in teams as if they were in a law firm. They rewrite a major contract and present their work to the rest of the class, as if the class were the client's CEO, CFO, and other senior managers. In all of this, students have to learn to operate on two modes. They have to ask two basic but competing questions: "What if?" versus "So what?" That is, they need always to be thinking about what they might be missing and what might go wrong, but at the same time, they need to ask if those issues are really relevant. Along the way, the students need to learn that the goal isn't to dump a lot of legal jargon on the client and show the client they are the smartest people in the room, unlike the normal classroom situation. Rather, they need to learn how to assess truly difficult legal issues and then how best to advise the client what to do, using language the client can understand.

I also ask the students to write an opinion letter that must address extremely difficult legal issues, but where they can't say, "on the one hand" versus "on the other hand." They have to come to a reasoned and supportable conclusion. This is the kind of rigorous and intellectually difficult process that happens inside a law firm, and there's no reason we can't this process while students are in law school.

Lisa Hart Shepherd

CHIEF EXECUTIVE
ACRITAS
NEWCASTLE UPON TYNE, UK

"Firms use our data to learn how to tailor their services to markets across the industry. We're helping them understand GCs better. We're helping them evolve and measure their performance with clients."

The company website describes Acritas as "the world's leading provider of legal market research." What's that mean?
I used to work in a law firm in the business world about thirteen years ago. I realized there was a vacuum in data on the legal market, so I combined market research with the law to help them with their legal planning. I started Acritas around 2002, and we launched Sharplegal, the annual survey, in 2006. Every year, we interview general counsel about the law firms they work with. Today, the survey has grown much larger and become more scientific. No other survey has global coverage of this scale across 45 countries.

How many GCs do you interview?

We interview 2,500 GCs every year. We ask about changes in their roles, changes in the market, changes in their legal spend, and changes in the geographic markets they need legal advice in. We ask what law firms they use, and we ask them to rate the firms in terms of performance. We ask who they're loyal to, what kinds of pitches succeed, and how pricing is changing and at what pace. GCs say one of the trends is they expect more substitution of legal-service providers and legal-process outsourcers for law firms.

How is the survey conducted?

The survey itself is a telephone survey. We have a call center in the UK with 25 full-time interviewers who speak ten different languages: French, German, English, Mandarin, Japanese, and so on. We break for a month, from the middle of December until the middle of January, and we reconvene and reshape questions in case we detect new themes or trends in the survey responses. Most questions remain the same, and sometimes we retire certain questions. If we've received the same result after 200 to 300 interviews, we have our answer, and we move on. One question was: "What was the best pitch you had from a law firm?" And the most common answer was that the firm didn't describe their firm's expertise in all areas. Instead, the firm proved that they understood the GC's business and described only the legal expertise that was relevant to that company.

Who buys the survey data?

Our clients who buy the data are law firms. We work with 30 to 40 law firms every year. We work with global firms like Freshfields. Some firms buy just the US data, but large firms buy our full global data set to understand how they perform in different markets. They use the data to learn how to tailor their services to markets across the industry. We're helping them understand GCs better. We're helping them evolve and measure their performance with clients. We've had a couple legal-process outsourcers and legal press interested in the data as well.

Did you start the company in response to demand?

We started the first year in the UK, because firms had come to us wanting to measure their brand recognition in the marketplace, but they didn't have money to do it robustly. So it grew from there. US customers wanted us to do it in the US market, so in our first year, we conducted surveys in the US and UK markets. Since then, we have rapidly grown our base of countries to 45.

How do you know what kinds of questions to ask?

My background was in market research before I worked at a law firm. So I knew about fast-moving consumer goods, and the complex relationships with insurance clients were similar to law firms. A lot of questions are open-ended. We created a lot of different ways to ask questions. We had five years of doing research for law firms and learning on the job before we set up the master survey.

Who writes the questions?

A team of people writes the questions. There is an interview team and a team of ten analysts and technical, research people. They draft, test, and redraft questions. We never share the questions, not even with our clients. It's been great, because we've been able to predict a lot of what has happened in the industry. We do a lot of qualitative interviews to refresh the design of the survey.

Have you been surprised by any findings?

There is a tendency to hype the amount of change going on in the market beyond actual reality.

GCs talked a lot about how they thought billing was moving to more alternative pricing and more work was moving to LPOs. They themselves weren't moving work or changing pricing, but they thought the market was. They said they preferred law firms to manage that kind of work for them. This didn't come through in the qualitative survey, but it did when we tested it in the broader market. The percentage of LPO work and alternative pricing hadn't changed at all.

We do a managing-partner survey. The firms that had a high proportion of work in alternative pricing were expected to move further in that direction, while firms who used alternative pricing in 10% of their work were expected to nudge a little more in that direction. But the fact was the general trend from 2010 to 2011 had hardly moved at all in the marketplace. The trend was stagnant.

We also asked our GCs if they'd worked in private practice. At the elite end, in the billion-dollar companies, about 74% of the GCs had worked in private practice, so that's how they understand pricing. They're comfortable with hourly billing. It's often the GCs resisting change in pricing. It takes work and discomfort to make a change. When demand picks up again, maybe we'll see more of a move toward alternative pricing.

The 2012 findings, however, reveal a step change in the need for change in the legal market. GC's are suddenly taking a much more aggressive stance on fee levels and efficiency. Perhaps an era of more radical change is finally upon us?

How was the fall of 2008?

Demand dropped in late 2008, and we suffered a 40% drop in revenue in 2009. But in 2010 we went up 60%, and we're back on our previous growth trajectory. I do find one thing very frustrating. We ask firms where they go for their intelligence, and most answer they're talking to peers or asking consultants. Very few say they buy or commission market research. This doesn't make much economic sense. It costs millions of dollars to open new firm offices, and they don't spend any time or money to research client demand and reduce their risk. Every other industry would have a research specialist or even a team. So firms have no data to back up their moves in the market and no way to tell good information from bad information. However, I do think this is changing, hence the growth in our revenue.

How are you marketing your business? How are you getting out there to persuade firms to buy your good research?

We build our brand by holding conferences and networking events. We have a sales team on the road taking meetings with CEOs and firms to educate potential clients about good and bad research. We advertise and receive a bit of press coverage, but we can't give away our data, because that's our business. We rely on recommendations, word of mouth, and people moving among firms. All of that helps.

Do you like the work you do now?

I'm glad I did it. It's great when clients use our data, but it's frustrating when a client says they don't know what to do with our data. They have to learn to think differently, and we have to educate them as much as we can. This work is more challenging than typical client-based work that lawyers are used to. This is more creative. We're learning all the time.

Do you think entrepreneurs like you are creating new kinds of jobs for law grads?

I'm helping more people in the business of law, as they go into management rather than into the legal or technical side of the law. We're helping provide intelligence to those people so they can do their jobs more effectively. We don't have any ex-lawyers on staff. People tend to be more research-oriented in our business. Some of our interviewers have studied law but never worked at a firm. They are actually working in a call-center environment and learning about clients and what clients want, which will give them great advantages when firms start hiring again.

Have you noticed any firms or LSPs altering their business models?

Some firms are changing. Some are using our research to change the way they work. They discover issues that surprise them, and they change their priorities and investments.

What do you see happening three to five years from now?

I think we'll broaden our survey and get more clients rating firms through us and giving us feedback. We will probably publish some of those results. We'll expand work in emerging markets so that our clients can understand how better to enter and work in those emerging markets. I think we will sell to firms in emerging markets. Our international clients are broadening their geographic footprint, so they want to understand those markets better. We already do a couple hundred interviews in China and Brazil, and I can see those numbers growing. There are about 35 very large cities in China, and law firms should know more about them.

What innovations would you like to see happening in firms and LSPs?

Two areas we highlighted two years ago were the rise of professional project management and the growth of alternative pricing, though pricing will take longer. Firms need to think harder about where they're positioned in the market. It's a hugely fragmented market, and firms will go through further consolidation. Most successful firms are very clear about their strategy. They know if they are a broad international practice or a boutique firm. The sooner they decide their position, the more successful they'll be. Trying to be all things to all people won't work.

Matthew K. Fawcett

SENIOR VICE PRESIDENT,
GENERAL COUNSEL, AND SECRETARY
NETAPP, INC.
SUNNYVALE, CA

"There are no stovepipes in our legal department. With great teamwork and association skills, we can see what others cannot and thus create value."

When did you start at NetApp and what were your initial goals?
I arrived at NetApp in September 2010. Our overarching goal is for the Legal team to help create competitive advantage for the Company. From that goal flows strategic objectives and tactical plans that we are carrying forward today.

What did you do before NetApp?
I was GC of JDS Uniphase. JDSU is a publicly traded technology-portfolio company, with a significant amount of business directed at telecom service providers and network equipment manufacturers, headquartered in Silicon Valley.

How did you make the move to NetApp?

I was not planning to leave JDSU, but when the opportunity arose at NetApp, I had to take a hard look. NetApp is a special company with a unique vision and strong culture. We are a growth company despite our multi-billion dollar size, and we are routinely recognized both as a great place to work around the world (#3 on the Great Place to Work Institute's "World's Best Multinational Workplaces" List and #6 on *Fortune Magazine*'s "100 Best" list) and as one of the world's most innovative companies (NetApp is the only storage vendor on *Forbes*'s List of the World's Most Innovative Companies).

How did you know how to hit the ground running at NetApp?

I had already built a playbook for how I would show up on Day One through my first year at a new company. I started creating it several years ago, because it helped me articulate and define priorities and expectations. It is essentially a huge spreadsheet of everything I believe a world-class legal department can and should do for its client. So, when I arrived at NetApp, I had a long task list "in the bag." As a shameless plug, I should add that the Association of Corporate Counsel (ACC), where I recently became a Director, has excellent materials on the role and scope of a GC, especially for new GCs.

Your objectives for Legal are not just cheaper and faster but better?

Our team, like lots of other legal departments, occupies a unique space inside the company. Our structure lets us see issues horizontally across all functions of NetApp, as well as vertically, from the Board room to individual contributors in distant geographies. There are no stovepipes in Legal. With great teamwork and association skills, we can see what others cannot and thus create value.

We spend a lot of time understanding and attaching to the Company's top corporate and functional goals. One goal is to innovate in every aspect of our business. It is easy to latch onto that for the legal department because, in my opinion, innovation will play a major role in our ability to create competitive advantage for NetApp.

How did your plan work out?

One of the nice things about writing a plan down is that you get to look at it later. At the 80/20 level, the agenda was right, and it was accomplished. Phase 1 has significant focus on the 3 Ps: people, purpose, and process. We have spent a lot of time restructuring the team, re-articulating a customer-focused strategy, and becoming process-focused where global consistency is key to scaling. Phase 2 shifts focus externally. We will spend more time developing relationships with ecosystem partners, taking on leadership roles in meaningful external associations, getting on the agenda of relevant agencies, regulators, and thought leaders, and helping demonstrate what makes NetApp a technology and community leader.

How have you dealt with technology in the legal department?

Technology will help us scale thoughtfully and will also help us create velocity in the business. To ensure focus on technology, the first big thing I did at NetApp was to create a new function, reporting to me, whose mission would be to develop and implement a long-term technology roadmap. Connie Brenton came in to lead the new Legal Operations department in the Fall of 2010. We have made great progress, and our best achievement to date is an e-contracting mobile app that has eliminated 1000 days of "wait time" for the global field sales team.

You won an award for innovation for your work in using Web 2.0 technology to foster communication among lawyers in all geographies.

Connie hired a team of tech-savvy, law-student interns who drove the platform project. They basically redesigned the legal-department's website—which was previously residing on multiple platforms. This puts us in a much better position to make real-time changes, is more dynamic and flexible than our prior platform, and will scale with the business. The intern team was terrific. They brought their knowledge of law and technology to the project, and a "no sacred cows" mindset that led us to creative results.

You're in a nice spot.

NetApp offers some of the most innovative technologies and solutions in the data-storage and management industry, which is squarely in the middle of exciting Big Data and cloud trends and is a company that cares deeply about culture and values. That is nice.

How are you tracking data?

Metrics matter...a lot. If you can measure it, you can achieve it; if you can't, you can't. We are trying to build fact-based measurements into our work, both in terms of data generated by our tools and technologies (for example, turnaround times and cost ratios) and by giving outside partners dashboard templates that have the data we would like to see from them, either on a quarterly basis or case basis.

What is the role of the GC in dealing with outside firms?

One of the factors behind NetApp's success for the past two decades has been the strength of its partnerships. I view our outside-firm relationships as fundamental to our success. As GC, I can help set the appropriate tone, fundamental relationship expectations, and success criteria. Our team of lawyers and professionals worldwide really has the big responsibility to select, retain, and manage (and terminate) outside partners within that framework.

Are law firms changing the way they do business?

I think they have to. I believe that the model driving law-firm profits is eroding. Where law firms could derive value before was charging for limited access to expensive, hard-to-get information. Now, the cost to obtain high-value data is often zero and cannot justify premium pricing. On top of that, the legal industry is seeing the explosion of new types of businesses (LPOs and e-discovery vendors being two prominent examples) that re-allocate work and expense more efficiently than before. The result has to be that traditional big-firm models cannot sustain over the long term. Mega-firm consolidations are perhaps a reaction to this trend, but it is not clear that these mega-mergers are the solution to these fundamental changes.

Michael Baroni

GENERAL COUNSEL
PALACE ENTERTAINMENT
NEWPORT BEACH, CA

"You have to proactively seek out change for the better. You can't wait for change to happen. You have to take action, implementing one project at a time."

What do you think about the state of the legal industry?
I've seen the legal industry dramatically change and law firms radically forced to reevaluate and legal departments turned on their heads. Only the people who innovate and look for new creative solutions will actually succeed in the industry.

Do you think these innovative people will come from inside or outside the law?
Innovators will likely come from within the legal industry itself, because these are the people most able to discern the fine-line details in need of improvement and to create new solutions. For example, Tom and Jeff Zuber [founders of the Zuber, Lawler & Del Duca firm in L.A.] recently invented LawLoop. I predict that will revolutionize the way law firms, legal departments, and all other sorts of businesses and companies communicate and

process their work—creating massive efficiencies and, therefore, improving in-house work performance and decreasing outside legal bills. LawLoop creates a "cloud" for communication that virtually wipes out the need for emails and spending endless time opening, saving, and filing documents.

But the bottom line for a general counsel is that there is no substitute for passion and energy and the ambition to accomplish things on the job. My entire career, I've never been trained by anybody. I came into my first in-house job and had to draw on what I learned in law school and internships, and I learned on my own every step of the way. You have to be an information maniac, ready to bull your way into challenges and proactively seek out change for the better. You can't wait for change to happen. Relentlessly ask yourself, "What more can I do to improve my job performance, the services I offer my in-house clients, and the company in general?" And then take action, implementing one project at a time.

Did you do anything differently during the 2008–2009 crisis?
Even in Orange County, that was a frightening time. Thousands of lawyers were rapidly laid off, and in-house legal-staff people were being slashed in a drive to cut costs. I'm aware of one fast-food company that cut their veteran general counsel and other legal staff, despite the fact that their revenues were rising.

I didn't do anything differently at that time, because I had already been doing everything I could to slash costs and maximize value for my client. For example, when I started at Bosch-Siemens [the world's third-largest home-appliance company, headquartered in Munich, Germany] in 2003 as their first North American general counsel, I immediately searched for ways to cut costs. The company had a retainer agreement for legal services, which they planned on keeping despite hiring me. They were paying millions of dollars a year, and yet in my opinion they were not getting their money's worth. So I killed a retainer arrangement and took on that work myself; that was an easy way to instantly realize significant savings.

I also looked for aggressive, smaller firms across the country with creative, hungry people who were client-oriented. Ironically, one of the most client-oriented attorneys I found was Jennifer

Moore, who—despite being with a very large firm [now a partner with Greenberg Traurig in Atlanta]—had more of that entrepreneurial spirit and approach to efficiently and creatively solving problems, rather than looking for ways to increase her billable hours.

One of the things I have done is to implement retainer agreements with fixed 20% discounts on hourly rates, and a refusal to pay for extraneous costs like legal research, overhead, secretarial overtime, and meals, and I structured flat fees on projects where appropriate. There were many times, for example, where I obtained project caps in the $2,000 to $3,000 range where the free-running, billable-hour fee likely would have generated a bill for five to ten times that amount. Unfortunately, larger law firms become experts at knowing how to take a simple matter and spin it twenty different ways to exponentially expand it into a sprawling project amongst associates and partners to create a mountain out of a mole hill. But if you pick the right firm, set clear expectations, and monitor them closely, then you can achieve better results at one-tenth of the cost.

How do you monitor outside counsel?
It's critical to have firms that are sincerely hungry to represent your business and to have firms that want to prove their worth to you every step of the relationship. You don't want firms luring you in with empty sales promises or taking you out to a nice restaurant and padding the bill to cover the restaurant charge and the time. I actually had a big firm that was courting me once, and I agreed to speak to the partner about certain antitrust issues to see if I could use him for future work. We had a nice 30-minute call, but a month later, I got a bill for several hours of his "preparation" time for the call, which included researching my client's business and how it applied to antitrust laws. That was just appalling.

On other occasions, I've asked a partner what seemed to be a simple legal question, and then I get a bill where the "simple" question has been researched by five associates, even though I never approved that. And you'll catch four or five people working on the same memo or responding to your email by copying three more associates—just so each of them can now bill you for "reading, reviewing and responding" to your email.

Other firms will take a contract you've asked them to review and edit, and instead of editing the contract, they will engage in massive commentary which simply throws several hours of questions back to you. This technique is used to purposely delay resolution of the contract, while forcing the general counsel into several rounds of endless discussions with the law firm and thereby exponentially spawning a wealth of billable hours.

These are examples of the schemes which many firms have devised to create systems which churn out more billable hours. They don't have any interest in providing efficient, problem-solving advice to the client. Their mindset is that the client is a billable-hours machine, and they try to rev that machine up and soak it for all it's worth. It's easy to spot this kind of mindset, and I refuse to utilize firms like that, which has saved my clients many millions of dollars while simultaneously getting better and swifter legal services.

How did you move from Bosch-Siemens to Palace Entertainment?

My true love is entertainment. I was ground up after six years at Bosch, working 80 hours a week as sole in-house counsel for a massive company. I desperately wanted to get back to entertainment and to find a positive and exciting environment. When you want a GC position, you can count on a year of hard searching. My focus was the entertainment industry, but I kept my options open. One of the worst things you could do is box yourself in. There may be great solutions out there that you foreclose unless you're open to them. But thankfully, I connected with Palace Entertainment, which is a dream. When your job is all about clean, family-fun entertainment, it brings that inner smile to you throughout your daily work. And I get to colorfully decorate my office with an array of amusement-park products and signs. Very fun.

What advice would you give today's law grads?

I see a lot of them approaching the job market in a narrow way. I've mentored students at Chapman School of Law, and I've given the students a presentation on résumés, to share what I look for in a candidate and how I weed out résumés. A résumé needs to get you in the door, so the most important thing is not to do anything which will give the reader an excuse to toss your résumé—and we sum up résumés visually in the first split second. If a résumé is jammed with tiny type, it immediately conveys that you can't concisely convey information. If the résumé is sloppily laid out, it tells me the person isn't organized. If there are typos and grammatical errors, you're not detail-oriented. And if your résumé states, "Objective: To utilize my bioengineering background," yet you're applying to a movie studio, you're just wasting your time.

I also tell people to leave no stone unturned. Ask everyone you know if they have a contact for you. Ask for five-minute informational interviews from any attorney who will give you an audience—and be gracious. Follow up with handwritten, old-fashioned thank-you notes. Be focused. Target employers in your chosen field which will be a good match with your experience—and direct it to a specific person. It's a waste of time to splatter your résumé to the wind, address it to "Dear Hiring Manager" or "Dear Human Resources," and hope something sticks.

In addition, you can't contact an employer just once. You need to follow up periodically. If I hadn't sent my résumé every two to three months to the same recruiter, I would have never gotten my first in-house job. That said, never hound someone—that's a huge turn-off to a person who is already stressed with job demands. Be brief, polite and cordial, and send a simple follow-up note every three months or so.

Recruiters and in-house attorneys turn to candidates who are impeccably organized, personable, polite and humble, and who, above all, send the signal that they will be trustworthy. We want people who will make our lives easier by being reliable. We run from people who send the signal that they will be lazy, egotistical, pushy, whiny, or demanding.

What did you do when you arrived at Palace Entertainment?
They had a GC before me, but he had a very different style and philosophy than I did. A lot of what I did in the beginning was just plain, old-fashioned, organizational clean-up. There were no corporate books, no contract system, no document-retention policy, no email policy, no social-media policy, no privacy policy, and virtually no contract forms. Corporate minutes and resolutions

were randomly piled in drawers and files, and it took me months of working weekends just to assemble them and get them into corporate books.

I had to redo all the liquor licenses and music licenses, file dozens of trademarks, establish a database for thousands of licenses and permits, and do a massive clean-up across eleven states to correct the proper company names. I created company organizational charts and a corporate history chart, which detailed the dozens of acquisitions and prior corporate entities. And I created books to catalogue all of the documents for each of the historical entities. I launched a "Safety First" campaign and established an Ethics Committee. So I really had to build a legal department from the ground up. I looked for ways to establish structure and catapult the level of legal services for my colleagues who were scattered across the country.

That's part of the challenge in a modern environment. When companies get turned over frequently, the paperwork turns into chaos, because everyone is focused on short-term goals and not on long-term stability. No one wants to put in the time to do fundamental, organizational projects which will benefit the company for many years to come. They just want do things for short-term recognition.

I'm the sole counsel for this company, which is the third largest in the world, with forty amusement parks. When I got here, I stepped back and asked, "How can I improve every part of the department and its interaction with each of the different amusement parks?" For example, with contracts, I did not want to review all contracts from forty different amusement parks. Instead, I created a stable of forms and taught the parks how to use them. Efficiency and legal protection dramatically increased. I began by emailing these forms, but I have been working on a long-term project to load all forms on an intranet, with instructions for each form. My goal is to design forms that are super easy for the business folks to use.

How do you communicate with people at forty parks?

It's always a challenge. Sometimes, I send memos to everyone to provide them with advice or guidelines. Sometimes we're all on a conference call. I often roll out new projects by sending one email to the entire group, and on individual park matters, I'm communicating via phone and email. We communicate by email, and I meet with all general managers to show them all the legal aspects of their work that apply to them: contracts, marketing, human resources, permits, government investigations, and so on.

When you bring work in-house, how do you keep staff trained?

At every company I've worked for, I've wiped out huge costs by bringing work in-house, but you can't do that unless you're obsessed with education and staying cutting-edge. I do as much as I can to be involved with Bar activities. I started an Entertainment, Sports, and Marketing law section for the Orange County Bar, and I'm a member of several sections at the O.C. Bar, including employment/labor, insurance, worker's comp, intellectual property, business litigation, and corporate law. You could pay firms to teach you, but the knowledge you soak up in an hour at a Bar activity is priceless. Legal knowledge changes rapidly, especially in labor law and product liability and human resources. Change has been dramatic. You're well served if you can keep a humble attitude. I'm never sure of what I know, and so I keep pushing myself to learn more. Reading articles is great, but it really takes getting more deeply involved. I'll typically do sixty hours a year of CLE.

What kinds of firms are you hiring for outside work?

In L.A., we've used Zuber, Lawler and Del Duca. They jump on a job. Those guys are a perfect example of zealous entrepreneurs. They are creative, bright, bursting with energy and enthusiasm, and serve the client. When I approached them with a major copyright-infringement case I wanted to pursue, they actually talked me out of it—which probably lost them a couple hundred grand in legal fees. But they don't care about inventing ways to generate fees. They care about doing such an honorable and superlative job that I will want to turn to them again and again as my most trusted counselors. And it's no surprise that they are growing fast and getting recognition. Tom Zuber is a perfect example of how, if you cater to clients, your reputation and business can fly.

How are you dealing with pricing?

I get pretty aggressive on pushing pricing issues. For instance, I promise certain territories to small firms, and I say, "I know your rate is $350 an hour, but if you do it for $190 an hour, I'll give you all personal-injury litigation in a particular state." We have truly phenomenal relationships with lawyers. We make the relationship as positive and mutually supportive as possible. You want to inspire them so that they love working for you. I use retainer agreements, and every firm that wants to work for us, across the board, they're going to give me a 20% discount.

When I came to Palace, for example, I saw our trademark work, and I felt that, while we were paying significant fees every month, it seemed that very little was actually getting accomplished. So I sent out an RFP for flat rates for trademark work, with a schedule of low, flat fees for all kinds of trademark-work activities. I chose a firm that was aggressive in low rates for TM work, but they also jumped on wanting our business. When you ask for proposals, some will answer in a day while others in a month, and that's an indication of how much they want your business.

How much did you save?

We cut our trademark bills in half, and yet we probably did twice the work. We started going after infringers and getting new trademarks. We now make sure to trademark the names of our parks, rides, attractions, and any special events, like Halloween or Christmas events. We had a lot of names that should've been registered decades ago. Some of our more famous parks had numerous infringers trading off our good name, and no one had ever pursued these infringers. That changed when I got to Palace. I have gone after every single one and, in the process, strengthened and protected our brands. In one case, there was a beer company that was using our park name; that can be damaging to your reputation, if people think that your family park has turned itself into a brewery.

How actively, as GC, do you oversee the work of your firms?

If you're not actively involved with managing firms and cases, you're going to have a process that fails. So with all firms, I say, "You can't outsource. I want to know how you're staffing projects, and I want to approve that staff." I'll speak with a partner about the issues coming up, and if an associate can handle part of a project, we'll agree to let him or her do it. But I also find that there is tremendous value when in-house staff works closely with outside counsel to prepare for cases and to brainstorm in general. On a number of cases we've taken to trial, for example, I'm convinced we have won them because of how closely I worked with outside counsel to rigorously prepare every detail and strategize.

Do you have any staff?
I have one paralegal, and she's a superstar. I don't want anyone on my team who isn't a superstar. When building a legal department, you have to surround yourself with people who are sharp and ambitious but who also possess great attitudes: people who are humble, professional, and respectful and who appreciate the good things about the job and the company they work for. You rely on the people who want to work and get things done and accomplish things. I also have a risk manager who handles insurance issues and worker's comp and who assists with litigation management. I have oversight of HR. And I have used legal interns from the Chapman School of Law, a relationship that is equally valuable for the department and the law student. The interns soak things up, even if they don't realize it.

How is the pace of work for you?
I typically work until 1 a.m. I stay at the office until 8 or 9 p.m., and I'll eat and stay up until 1 a.m. There's always a huge mountain of work raining over my head. I just try to prioritize and not get stressed about all the work that is waiting to be attended to. As a GC, you have to be proactive with projects that can ultimately save people time or shield liabilities. You can't sit there and just do work that comes to you that day. You have to stay ahead of the game.

How much of your work is communication?
During the day, you're dealing with big-ticket items, like litigation, landlord disputes, and contract negotiations, and you need to talk with law firms and all your colleagues. But at night I can plow through all the heavy work without interruption.

How do you define value?

Keeping costs low for the in-house legal department while delivering superior value, keeping outside legal fees extremely low while obtaining the absolute best representation, and shielding the company from liabilities while simultaneously constantly working to improve the company in whatever way possible. Being a GC means you try to make other people's work easier and more effective by being a problem-solver and a facilitator.

I undertook a benchmarking study, and in some ways, it was very difficult to compare. Statistics can always be misleading and hard to come by. But I knew we were having great results in the legal department, and I wanted to show the CEO. No matter how much money we save, whatever we spend on legal liabilities is still money out the door.

What I spent, total, in 2010 was what our competitors spent on a single litigation case. Our competitors spent about 3% of company revenue on outside litigation fees, verdicts, and settlements. We spent about .75% of company revenue. And that's with comparable companies in our line of business. Our legal department is extremely lean for a company with forty amusement parks. Other comparable companies have far larger departments. Our internal legal costs are .25% of company revenue, while competitors spend about .5% to .75% of company revenue on internal legal costs. So we're at a half or a third of others.

Again, it's difficult to benchmark, because no one wants to share their litigation and insurance information. But I was able to get some information from certain places. The average litigation cost is about $250,000 per case. We spend, per claim, $35,000 to $50,000 for all legal fees, plus settlement. Our settlement value is approximately 10% of what companies are being sued for.

How do you see yourself taking advantage of technology in the coming years?

The best way to take advantage of technology is to have talented IT professionals in-house who can customize technological solutions that fit your exact needs. I'm wary of large databases from third-party providers, however, because if you don't set them up 100% accurately and monitor them, the whole thing becomes useless. And these outside tech companies make more money fixing the databases and services they sell you than they do selling you the "solution" in the first place! I'm sure the technology platforms help some organizations, but I'm wary of them. In addition, technology is no substitute for continuing to give your attention to legalities. If you end up relying on certain technologies, instead of focusing on direct contact with people, then you often undermine what you're trying to accomplish. Technologies aren't a magic pill.

.

Richard A. Matasar

VICE PRESIDENT FOR
UNIVERSITY ENTERPRISE INITIATIVES
NEW YORK UNIVERSITY
NEW YORK, NY

"The world we live in means that, at the end of three years, students have to go out and get a job. Clients want faster, cheaper, better from law firms, and students want that from law schools as well."

Did you do anything differently during the 2008–2009 crisis?
From 2007–2008, the biggest change was the financial climate of New York City. A year before the Lehman Brothers collapse, there was already a significant impact in the bond market in New York. Municipal, not-for-profit bonds—all were showing signs of market weakness. It was an important signal to higher education and law schools that financial conditions were changing, and it was a precursor signal that there were weaknesses in the economy. Our antennae were up. The job offers going out to law grads in 2006–07 were already softening. Firms were asking students to start late. Finally, with the collapse of Lehman, there was an impact on the legal market, and law firms were rescinding offers.

It forced all of us thinking about student outcomes and students' likely job prospects to become worried in a different way than before. The aftermath suggested this was not symptomatic of a typical downturn but was evidence that something was fundamentally broken in the market. We had to start thinking about preparing law grads to enter the market with different mindsets, as self-starters, open to alternative practices, being entrepreneurial, and so forth.

There were downturns in '87 and during '91 to '94, but those downturns were temporary. The worse the economy was, the more applications there were for law schools. A bad economy drove more people to apply to law school. The mindset was, "If you graduate from college with few prospects, then you return to school for more training and education in order to expand your prospects." But that didn't happen in 2008. There was reticence in students looking at legal education in terms of whether they wanted to take on the risk of more debt for higher education. Legal education was becoming a risk. Debt was a financial risk, and their prospects were cloudy. So there were fewer applications. I'd been predicting this since '93. I wrote this back then. This informed our planning at New York Law School, where we'd been thinking for a while in terms of lower applications.

The biggest growth period of law schools and law students came after the Viet Nam era. I became a dean in 1991. Since that time, there has been a steady growth in enrollments across the academy, driven both by increased enrollment in long-standing schools and new enrollment in new schools. By the time we hit the downturn in 2008, enrollment was up a couple thousand from just a decade earlier. So the number of grads had gone up, not down, and applications were substantially higher in 2008 than a decade earlier. From 2008 to 2012, schools experienced real change for the first time. First, there was a big decrease in applications, not necessarily in enrollment, because there have always been more applicants than slots. More recently, enrollments have decreased as schools have sought to maintain quality. The real question is how much deterioration is yet to come.

If someone were on the fence about going to law school today, what would you advise?

In the '90s, students made a rational choice: if they didn't know what to do, they went to law school. It was a good option. But in the last few years, the number of students who have gone to school because they don't know what else to do has gone down, especially as family's resources have gone down. If you go to school on the mom-and-dad loan, it's an attractive option. Law school is only three years, it's useful, and the state gives you a monopoly to do something you couldn't otherwise do.

And your writing will get better. The quality of writing is significantly higher among lawyers than the general population. It's interesting to watch that "A-ha!" moment with a student when they walk in the door. As a law professor, I ask them to write what they did during the summer. And then I ask them to write about a case, and I compare the two pieces and ask, "What happened to your clear writing?"

The discipline of a legal education can be incredibly useful across disciplines when you graduate. If law school costs little, or if you have money, it's a great choice. If you're in the middle and you don't have support resources, it's a bigger risk.

What trends should law schools respond to, in terms of designing education for incoming law students?

Most law schools and legal educators focus on the substance of law. They focus very little on emerging trends in the profession. They focus on their fields. It's a prescriptive business. The descriptive part is: *this is what the world looks like now.* The prescriptive part is: *this is what the world* should *look like.* When you think about your legal studies, you stay up late at night and talk about this stuff. This is great. But the world we live in means that, at the end of three years, students have to go out and get a job. So there's a transition of academic study into the vocational part of law, from school to work. Clients want faster, cheaper, better from law firms, and students want that from law schools as well.

And this is not just true for law schools. It's true for all higher education. Students are looking to get more out of school without spending more money and without staying longer. There's a strong push for change in the legal-education business, but there's a tremendous pull from the client/practice side saying we have to train students better. Schools have to serve the needs of students first, and that means we have to recognize the demands of the employment world the students want to enter.

What about apprenticeship programs for law students?

There's not a sweet spot for apprenticeship in law school. Third-party payers support clinical faculty in teaching hospitals, but there's no equivalent method in legal education for externalizing the costs of training. They are borne internally by the law firm and the law school or else by the graduate.

There's literature on expertise and becoming an expert, and most of the literature finds that a person needs ten years to become an expert. Law school is only three years. So you need another method, a robust training system after school: in work, in trial and error, and in practice.

How is legal education responding to trends in technology?

You have to disaggregate learning to figure out the best way to deliver learning. The first thing that happens in a classroom is that professors deliver information to students simply by telling it to them. That kind of delivery of pure information can be disaggregated. In fact, you can take the professors who are excellent at giving lectures, and they can deliver that information to hundreds of students.

But that's not everything. The second thing in the classroom is that students prove they've read the material and know something. That's where the professor gets up and does a gut-check. The professor asks a few, randomly selected students if they've read the material and know the facts of the case. That's pretty inefficient. Every student could prove that online by passing a quiz or demonstrating their knowledge by answering questions.

The third thing is professors try to provide expert guidance and wisdom to students, to see connections where students can't see them. That should be done—and can only be done—in smaller groups, seminars, independent studies, and mentoring relationships.

If you find a way to mechanize the first two things in the classroom—delivering information and quizzing individual students on that information—then you're going to see, in law school and higher education, a trend toward the third thing—that is, professors working with smaller groups of students. A disaggregation of classroom instruction enables the professor to focus on teaching at the level of individual students and very small groups.

How does this shift the emphasis of what law schools are going to do?

Knowledge is free. You have libraries and the internet. Lectures are going to be delivered as recorded videos or done live online. Many schools have online courses, but MIT, Stanford, and others are posting some courses on the web for free. You can learn calculus online, for free. However, if you want someone to know that you've gained that knowledge—that is, if you want the degree—that costs a lot: $50,000 or more. As technology becomes more seamless, ubiquitous, in your pocket and on your desktop, we'll have easy access to great lecturers who can say lots of important things about important stuff. The lectures may be cheap and mass-produced, but that will likely improve with time. The main thing is you won't get certification or one-on-one instruction time. So you will get the information, but you may not understand it.

At New York Law School, we pioneered project-based learning. It's an exercise that comes to students in a small class, no more than eight students. The challenge is to answer a specific, client-driven or world-driven problem. We align it with faculty research. A faculty member is doing something interesting, like, for example, writing a new federal rule, and the students would do this project, and write up a new rule. That's a very lawyer-centric activity. That's what lawyers do, and this pedagogy puts students into an environment where they have to work together. And students learn about something real—a publication, a document, a policy, etc.—and it could be something open to review by outsiders, if it's published online or elsewhere. And they have to be accountable as a team and work to deadlines. They have to manage the project.

This is not litigation-oriented. It's problem-solving oriented. Litigation can be a portion of what lawyers do, but problem-solving is what they always do.

What is your role now?

My role now is to rethink education starting from high school until college. I think of alternative delivery systems for education: online, disaggregated from time and space, courses in New York and London and California. Can you start college in high school? Can you start graduate education in college? Also, I consider ways to incubate ideas. I'm trying to make college education better, faster and cheaper.

When you talk about the value of college to students, you tell them they get better value in their lives for what they spend on college. You tell parents that, for the cost of tuition, students start on their paths to their dreams. In the education world, it's difficult to talk about this, because the way things have been done are changing. My role is to translate new ideas into ways that feel comfortable for the people—professors and administrators and students—who are already working within the existing system.

How do you encourage people to change?

Most people recognize that change is good for society, as long as *they* don't have to change. Very few people I know embrace the idea that every day is a new challenge and are prepared to work outside their comfort zone. Faculty members are experts, and it's not fun for them to hear that they need to change the way they're doing things, even just a little. The teaching portion of what we do becomes simpler over time. The longer you do something, the more you refine the process over the years to become easier. And so it's not a simple thing to say to this person that their efficient methods have to change to benefit the learner. That happened in law firms. Clients were no longer willing to pay law firms to support so many associates. Firms had developed their systems over decades, and now they had to change in response.

Sometimes people retire rather than change. Or if you're in a position where people can't fire you—say, you have tenure—you can refuse to change. Law firms who used to get along by saying they're the best and most expensive have to face the fact that here come firms just as good but cheaper, and now they have to change to compete. This is happening in law schools as well.

Do you think change will come quickly to law schools?

The pace of change has never been faster than it is right now, and I can't see that it will slow down in the future. Not all sectors will change at the same pace. At the high end of law-firm practice, where deep-pocket clients demand service at any price, you won't see a lot of change. At the lower ends, where people are beating each other up in competition, you'll see a lot of change. Unlike in the UK where there is a strong subsidy for education even to this day, our American education market requires that families pay, and so you'll see faster change here because families will demand it. Change won't happen too quickly in law schools, because of the ABA and regulations, and it won't be too responsive to market pressures, but other parts of higher education will change very quickly.

How different does the university look today than it looked a hundred years ago? It's pretty different. In twenty years, I'm guessing the university will change more significantly than in the last hundred.

Are the students in law schools different today, in terms of, say, how accustomed they are to getting information from easily accessible technology?

When I was a kid (and even until the mid-1970s), you had four or five things to choose from on TV, and if you missed a show, you couldn't see it for six months. If you wanted to watch something at two a.m., you were out of luck. The VCR and Beta shifted that. I would suggest that our interaction with screens is completely different today than when I was a kid. Back then, we were passive recipients of entertainment created by others, but today, we menudrive our own interests and choose our own entertainment at will, on demand. I really think because change is happening while we're experiencing it, it does not feel too disruptive. It's more of a progression of technologies. We can do things we didn't know we wanted to do, and we adapt so quickly that we can't imagine not doing them. The first portable cellphone was the size of a briefcase, and now a smartphone is more powerful than the computer you had five years ago. I think that absolutely this changes people. So over time, these small changes accumulate into significant differences.

Here's an exercise. Sit with your extended family in the living room. Watch what the kids eighteen and younger are doing. Everyone is on their own machines. I saw this with my own nieces and nephews. They were playing Scrabble on their smartphones, playing each other during conversations, with the TV going. That's different. I don't know if it's better, but it's different. And it's not going away. We have to understand the shifting culture of the people who are the workers of tomorrow. It's difficult to tell incoming law students that everything they've done for the last twenty-two years of their lives is irrelevant, and they have to do things like their grandparents did. They will refuse to do things like their grandparents or even parents did. That's not going to work. We just cannot predict what will be retained from the old and what will be adopted from the new.

How do you define value?
You have to think about return on investment and consider short-term value versus long-term value. Typically, people want immediate gratification. We want return on an investment in one day. We want to get stronger the first day we exercise. We want to be guaranteed that we'll lose fifty pounds in a month, or we won't even start.

So if you look at legal education in the short term, you have a hard time measuring value. If you measure legal education solely in terms of the average starting salary after graduation, then the value of law school depends on the salaries going up or down in the market. If lawyer salaries go down, then the value of law school is perceived as going down. That's a math problem: lower salary equals lower return on investment, and that equals *bad*.

So you have to see intrinsic value in knowledge and wisdom and growth. You have to take into account that you will become a better person, and your mind will be capable of doing things you couldn't have done before. You will be a better citizen, a more effective participant in business and society.

These more abstract but intrinsic values of critical thinking have value over time in someone's life and in the quality of our culture. So we work with students and society to say there is intrinsic value in knowing and being better at things. Then you weigh the value of the long-term return. Higher education is better for everyone, because you will become better. We have to look at the long-term value proposition.

So ideally, education transforms people and offers people an opportunity to transform themselves.

There's a transformative nature to participation. I use a basketball metaphor. I maxed out at my height at fourteen years old. A coach told me, "You can't teach height." How do you explain Adrian Dantley, 6'5", who'd been the best rebounder in the NBA? You *can* teach boxing out and rebounding. As educators, we can teach students to make the most of what they have. As long as that's still true—and we have the ability to add value as teachers and bring people together to learn from each other—we can add tremendous value, regardless of what people bring to the table.

Society rewards hard work more than school does. Merely working hard is not enough when you're relatively ranking your students on one variable, their cognitive abilities. The world rewards people for more than their cognitive abilities: personality, networking, stick-to-it-iveness. To the extent education doesn't recognize those values, educational success underpredicts people's success in the real world. My job is to start optimizing those values in education.

Hugh Totten

PARTNER
VALOREM LAW GROUP, LLC
CHICAGO, IL

"We figured there was a market opportunity for lawyers who took skin in the game. Like most entrepreneurs, we wanted to be a for-profit entity, but we wanted to do it by creating new opportunities for cost-savings and risk-sharing with our clients."

What was the seed of inspiration for starting Valorem?

After I graduated from law school in 1985, I clerked for a year for the chief federal judge in Chicago and then decided to join Kirkland & Ellis' Chicago office. It was a big firm by the standards of its day (I was lawyer 300-something), but it had a litigation swagger much like the old Oakland Raiders football team. "Just Win, Baby," seemed to be the prevailing ethos. Knowing essentially nothing about the business of law (or anything beyond litigation, or even any real-life lawyers), I went into litigation. At the time, it seemed like the choice was a simple one that opened more doors than it closed. I never expected to stay long, but over time that turned into never expecting to leave. But leave I did, in 2003, because after 18 years, the firm and I had grown, and grown apart. As it turned out, it was a key event along the path to eventually forming Valorem. I loved the money, but I wanted more freedom and flexibility. More than anything, I wanted to know that my partners had my back and weren't trying to stick knives in it. K&E is a great firm with great lawyers, but its culture back then resembled the Italian nation-states before the unification.

After considering the options, I left Kirkland Ellis at the end of 2003. I talked to a number of firms, including Butler Rubin where I met Pat Lamb. Pat is his own force of nature. He knew he couldn't get me to Butler, and we talked about starting our own firm. Instead, I decided to join Perkins Coie, a Seattle-based firm that was opening an office in Chicago. It presented the opportunity to work for a collegial firm with a national presence as well as the unique opportunity to help build an important office to serve such major clients as Boeing, which had just moved its headquarters to Chicago. Working with a close friend there with whom I had worked previously at K&E, the office grew from 30-some lawyers to over 70. I found the business of law as exciting and interesting as the practice of law. Eventually, I figured I could do that same thing for myself and have an even better time.

So you reconnected with Pat Lamb to see if he was still interested in starting a new firm?

Yes. We had been connecting here and there for lunch and the like and talking about what it would be like to have our own firms. The "A-ha!" moment came as a result of volunteering to be on a technology committee at Perkins. I met with major vendors of electronic-discovery software and services. We met over a multi-day period. This led me to think about industry trends and what was going to happen in the future.

Eventually, I was asked to give a presentation to litigators in the firm in 2006 at the annual meeting in Phoenix. I talked about technology and industry trends, such as outsourcing to India and technologies that would make delivery of legal advice faster, simpler and cheaper. I wondered where computer technology would take us, but the reception I received wasn't what I would call enthusiastic. Lawyers can be an incremental bunch, and that got me thinking about where I was going to be in 10 to 15 years.

Pat Lamb and I kept talking, and we decided to take the opportunity to ride this wave and be entrepreneurial. We wanted to bring business discipline to the moribund industry we're in. You never see a lawyer in the business section at Barnes & Noble. For years, lawyers haven't had to be disciplined. Lawyers have ridden a wave of incredible success, and the biggest of the AmLaw 100 have had so much success that some would argue it's turned into excess at the expense of their clients. We wanted to serve clients and partner with them; we figured there was a market opportunity for lawyers who took skin in the game. Like most entrepreneurs, we wanted to be a for-profit entity, but we wanted to do it by creating new opportunities for cost-savings and risk-sharing with our clients. We wanted to focus on client needs, and we have been evolving our concept over a period of years.

The crash of 2007–08 made the entire industry think about alternative fees, and suddenly everyone claimed to offer them. But what we've found over the years is that big law firms tend to quote an alternative fee by first looking at the number of billable hours they will incur. They engineer the risk out of the alternative fee, because their inherent billable-hour basis builds in a profit margin that most businesses can only dream about. Surprisingly, we also found that clients have a skepticism about alternative fees. When you sit across the table from them, you can tell they're thinking to themselves, "How am I going to get screwed by this?"

We've dealt with that in several ways. We always quote several alternatives, so the client can choose what risk profile is most comfortable. And we include a "value adjustment box" on each invoice where clients can write the bill down as they see fit. We obviously don't want to see that happen, but when it does, it serves as an early warning signal that adjustments in many ways have to be made.

When exactly did Valorem become reality?

There were three of us in January 1, 2008, and we were joined a few months later by a fourth. Mark Sayre in L.A. came with Pat. They'd tried many cases together. Mark works in L.A. and runs part of our practice there. Nicole Auerbach was one of the 40 most influential people under 40 in a magazine in Chicago. She had worked with Pat at Katten and wanted to be entrepreneurial, so she joined us in April of 2008. It's been a great ride ever since. Today there are eleven of us. We have five partners, three of-counsels, and three associates.

How do partners and associates work together at Valorem?

Our associates have a great deal more responsibility than their peers in law firms. They're taking depositions. They play roles in cases immediately. We're so small that the training they get daily is far more than they would receive at any Big Law firm. *Valorem* means "value," and everyone has to contribute some value to the process. As partners, we also do a lot of our own work, because it's more efficient. After twenty-seven years, I know what a key document is, and I know evidence rules. I write most of my briefs from scratch and bring associates to fill it in, rather than the other way around. I have a 25-point memo for my associates on how I write briefs and how to work with me. And we train them in that regard, because we want them to be not just efficient but better advocates. We notice—all of us main partners having come from large firms—that the kids coming out of law school do not know how to advocate. They write briefs in which they explore issues from all points of view, but those briefs serve no purpose for a litigator. A litigator has to be a strong advocate. We write our briefs as strong advocates for our clients, because that's what they're paying us for.

Do you have the typical office set-up, or did you do something different there, too?

Our main office is in Chicago. We wanted a building that represented traditional values, but we wanted space that didn't look like a conventional law firm. We ended up in a building built in 1927. We took two upper floors, and we have 11,000 square feet. We have glass walls, small offices, and bigger collaborative spaces. Our offices look like a software-engineering campus. And we wanted that effect. We wanted to break the mold, in our office and in our working model.

Unlike law firms that fight every year over compensation, we don't have those fights. We have the Camelot system. Everybody is paid the same, and we all share in the firm's successes and burdens. That means when I have a client who needs help, my partners are there, and I'm not afraid that my partners will steal my client. In large firms, they talk about the supermarket of different legal talent, and there is always talk about "cross-marketing," but there's always the fear that a colleague will claim another's revenues. That's sort of a shame, because it fails to build on the natural synergies that having partners provides. We didn't want that result. We wanted the benefit of collaboration and bringing different points of view to each problem. You have to take each other's back. I can step in on a case and help, and my colleague shouldn't have to worry about me taking over their case. Never again did we want to sit in on a compensation meeting. Those meetings are the single, most destructive force driving law firms to be incredibly inefficient.

We wanted to promote collaboration not only because it results in a "better" product, but it also is the wave of the future as this profession morphs into lawyers being trusted advisors as well as knowledge professionals. The United Kingdom is leading the way on this now, having opened up law-firm ownership and management structures to non-lawyers. So much of what lawyers do is simply solve problems that are not so simple and that involve many disciplines.

For example, I sit on an advisory board for a major university, and I find myself in amazement when I listen to my fellow board members talk about the problems their clients face and how they solve them. The other board members might be in PR or distribution or whatever, but they are using many of the same management tools we are. And they are selling, essentially, what we sell—trust and wisdom.

Legal-industry clients are willing to pay a lot of money for trust and wisdom, but they're not so willing to pay for the training needed to obtain either. That's the challenge that will face the legal industry over the next generation. It can only be solved by bringing in people with different expertise and perspectives and re-tooling our training model, from the law school up. When you think about it, we're simply reversing the trends of the last century and returning to an apprentice-like model.

Do you bill hourly?

Yes, because that's what some clients want. It's how clients grew up in the profession, and they sometimes feel more comfortable understanding a time-based, task-based billing system. So if that's how a client wants to be billed, we'll do it, but we also will present several options. We hope to help clients understand that the hourly rate is based upon a 100-year-old time study originally performed for laborers in the factory setting. Translating the time it takes to lift and tote really has no correlation to the time it takes to develop an effective strategic analysis. Indeed, time- and task-based billing didn't really get much attention in the legal profession until the late 1950s, when the ABA published a study encouraging lawyers to bill based upon time spent because doctors had been so successful in selling procedures based upon the time it took to perform. Many lawyers held out for many years for the old system of billing for value. I remember some of the first bills I saw go out in the 1980s were one-page long and said, in sum total, "For services rendered," and then provided an amount.

For whatever reason—transparency, good client relations, whatever—clients, mostly large insurance companies, thought they could control legal spend by insisting on small-increment billing, especially in commodity-type cases where one case is essentially the same as the previous one. So we have this system where you get down to tenths of an hour, literally six-minute increments. Who thinks or acts in six-minute increments? Nobody. It's absurd, and it's even more absurd for a third-party to come in and fight over whether it should have taken six minutes or twelve to perform a task.

So in many ways we have returned to the virtues of the past, when you sent a bill for services rendered. Then, it was an after-the-fact determination by the lawyer about what value his services provided. Today, it's an upfront discussion and agreement between lawyer and client about that value, with perhaps a performance kicker. The test is not how much you can squeeze monthly from your client, but how long clients stay with you because you're a trusted advisor who provides value.

I talk about disaggregating services in law-firm work. On the litigation side, the law firm typically engages in as many pretrial services as possible, and they tend to panic as the case nears trial. Many litigators never try a case, or they try very few. Ninety-nine percent of these cases don't go to trial. So what's the point of drawing up a budget that includes going to trial if you know you're not going to trial? What's the point of paying a firm to review documents when statistics show that associates reviewing those documents make errors in one out of every five pages? You have a 20% error rate, and you're paying enormous sums of money. We want to take a realistic valuation of the case and of our ability to win it.

How do you talk about value with your clients?
We're in educational mode, because GCs who came from law firms conceive of their role as a consumer buying units by the hourly increment. So we have to get GCs thinking differently about value for the first time. Some, like Jeff Carr of FMC Technologies, are way ahead of the game. Mark Chandler of Cisco is another.

The first thing I do is ask a client, "If you could sit down with the other side right now and resolve this on a business-to-business basis, what would the deal terms look like?" Most clients who have been sued or are thinking about bringing a suit have no real answer when they come to me. Many want to fight every fight and pick up and throw every rusty nail. For a litigator who bills by the hour, that works great—for a while. But, as the monthly bills pile up, clients eventually realize that there is an economic tipping point where every incremental dollar spent on the litigation brings with it an increasing pain. I try to get clients to envision what victory means and what the clearest and shortest pathway is without chasing into every dark alley or rabbit hole.

This requires the client to think about value as a concept—what is valuable to them, what is valuable to the other side, and how do we envision a value that everyone can benefit from? Clients have to, and most do, understand that, unlike appraising, which has generally recognized standards and techniques, there is both art and science to understanding litigation value, but we can still draw from the lessons appraisers have used to become more scientific in their approach. For example, the appraisal field has many different concepts of value, not just "fair value" or "fair market value," but values for different purposes, including accounting accuracy and *ad valorem* taxes. Many clients do this internally when they set their reserves for contingent losses. We just want to make it an upfront and collaborative process where litigation is viewed as an asset or liability just like any other intangible right owned by the business.

Once a client puts an appropriate value on a case as an asset or a liability, the next decisional element is how much to spend to protect the asset or guard against the liability. Litigation for most businesses is an investment just like any other investment—except you're ultimately asking twelve strangers off the street to decide your fate. That's not a business model most businesses are comfortable with.

Of course, there are a number of factors that make it difficult to come to an agreement about value. If someone's being sued, they're acting under duress. This is not a classic buyer/seller relationship. They need something urgently when they buy it. But lawyers don't price services. They engage in conscious parallelism: they charge what other firms are charging. They don't charge according to the value of their services or to the market. And I always shy away from the client who first approaches me and says, essentially, "I want to hire the biggest asshole lawyer I can find and make the other side squirm." That almost always leads to very expensive litigation and client regrets.

Firms can try better to understand their objectives and the implications for success and failure. Sometimes that can go case by case, but until the client sits down and goes through the exercise of what their objective is, how they can achieve it, and how they can assess the financial impact, you get very different views on the value of a piece of litigation. For example, maybe a lawyer changes something to increase the revenue of the company, so maybe the lawyer should get a cut of that increased revenue. That's how advertising firms billed in the early 1960s. That's largely disappeared now, but the point is that you have to partner with clients on risk and reward. We take on performance incentives, because that's where you get the value of lawyering. You don't get the value of lawyering when you're indifferent to the result.

Are these performance incentives the equivalent of bonuses for good outcomes?

Outcomes have determined lawyers' fees for generations. Plaintiffs' personal-injury lawyers have worked on a performance-incentive basis for many years and still do. There's no reason it shouldn't happen on the other side of the "versus" sign. Here's a good example. We had a client company that manufactured a breakthrough product, and they were in a dispute with a distributor. The client didn't want to spend a whole lot of money on lawyers, but this was a very important case for them. So we took a reduced hourly rate that had a performance kicker payable in stock warrants once the company goes public. We did a good job. We got a good result. And we ended up with stock warrants of a company that we hope will be very valuable one day.

Are you unbundling services?

Yes, this is an absolute priority. We are working with Novus Law LLC in Chicago on joint client development. Novus Law has developed a Six Sigma process for reviewing documents and getting them ready to hand over to litigators in a pre-packaged, "here's the story" way, and the cost is forty- to sixty-percent less than what clients typically pay a large law firm for simple document review. We don't want to make our money off document review. We want to make money off what we can leverage, our talent and wisdom. Our business model depends on our ability to disaggregate and ramp up and down as we see fit, with our operations centered on our core group of people. We can be far more efficient doing it that way.

Do you assemble different bands of people case by case?

I've worked on valuation disputes for different national parks: Grand Canyon, Yellowstone, the Statue of Liberty, and Lake Mead. In the Statue of Liberty case, we had a valuation dispute arising from a contract involving a fleet of Circle Line Boats that went to the Statue of Liberty. In that case, we outsourced legal research to India on certain issues, and we brought in contract staff for document assembly, review, and production. We have also had cases in which we've taken on much greater risk that a large firm would take. We took a large fraud case where I was representing a bankruptcy trustee, and I turned over client documents knowing there was nothing privileged. I didn't review those documents, because my fraud case depended on what was in the other guy's documents. Firms don't turn over documents like that, because they make money reviewing documents even when they don't need to.

Did you do anything differently at Valorem during the crisis of 2008 to 2009?

We haven't tinkered with our model since we opened. We thought then that the great recession was going to move people into our space. Instead, they've still been fighting it and looking to return to what was normal. The old lions in law firms are fighting this tooth and nail. People are saying we're getting back to normal after the recession, but this is a new normal.

If we stay in denial, we're all going to wake up one day and be out of business. We're not going to get our asses kicked by crony capitalism or cheap labor in China. It will be because young people here are willing to challenge "the rules" and are fearless about delivering services in a totally different way. They are not hidebound to the ways things have been done. They're willing to try anything. That's the cost of living in a flattened, crowded world.

Why do you think lawyers have been slow or unwilling to change?

The legal industry has the wrong idea about creativity. Creativity today doesn't play by the rules. You throw the rules out and start from scratch. We're dealing with fundamental changes. In this profession, there are times when there's nothing more miserable than dealing with other litigators. We have a very high asshole factor in this industry, and it is shameful, sometimes, that the level of discourse and everyday dealings are where they are. It's not hard to understand why people hate lawyers. Dealing consistently with them makes the job difficult.

One of the things that invigorates you after twenty-seven years is running your own shop and fearing you might fail. When we started this place, we wanted to build it up by building blocks. Then a book came out a year later called *What Would Google Do?* And it was what we were doing. We were applying those principles to how we put together a law firm. To most business people, all this is normal. It's competition on value, and it doesn't hide the ways we deliver services. We don't curse technology. We embrace it, because technology makes us more efficient, and we deliver that value to clients. We embrace collaboration because it makes us better.

What do you think about innovation in legal education?
Law schools have to teach kids and train them so they're better prepared to be knowledge workers in a hugely crowded field. Students need better value for the enormous amount of money they're spending. Schools should be responsible for what they're doing, not just turning out one graduating class after another using the same old instructional methods.

At the University of Miami Law School, I participated in something called "Law Without Walls," orchestrated by Michele Beardsley and Michael Bossone. The project brings together professors, professionals, investors, MBA-types, entrepreneurs, and students in online meetings. The students and participating professors are from schools all across the globe, including Oxford and the Peking Law school. We meet initially somewhere in the world in January and assign topics to groups of students on, essentially, the business of law and the challenges facing the profession, such as improving access to justice. We then meet each week, all of us, online using Adobe Connect Pro. Guest lecturers join us and talk about current industry issues. The students then work together in groups to develop an idea for a business, be it for-profit or nonprofit, and work with their practitioner mentors and professors to develop a business plan. Students are paired internationally so they get used to working globally and with different cultures.

In April, we all meet in Miami, and the students give 45-minute presentations about the ideas that they have developed. We invite investors and entrepreneurs to judge each presentation as though it is a presentation to a company's board of directors. I was picked because of what we were doing in billable-hour/alternative-fee spaces. It is like a business boot camp for the law students, and their ideas are both fascinating and refreshing. One year, my students came up with a prescient idea to develop an eBay-type service to purchase certain routine legal services. You start with the sale of residential properties, and attorneys bid on what they would charge to represent consumers in different markets. It's kind of a reverse auction. Two weeks later, I read in the *ABA Journal* that somebody was doing this and funding a website to host it. Those are the types of things we love to get involved in. It's that kind of new thinking that will drive the legal profession, and we just want to be a part of it.

Look ahead three to five years, and talk about your business and the industry.

Bill Gates once said that we over-predict the amount of change that will happen in two years and under-predict the amount of change that will happen in ten. Here are the things I think are going to begin happening in 3 to 5 years.

1. The services that lawyers provide will in many ways be seen as almost interchangeable with the services provided by other knowledge professionals. As a result, firms will arise that consist of lawyers and many other owners who have a variety of backgrounds and disciplines to provide more of a strategic consulting where advising about the law will be just one component. This is already being allowed in the United Kingdom. Indeed, Australia has permitted Slater & Gordon to issue shares to the public, which is likely to happen in the United States in the long run, not by successful defense firms, but by plaintiff firms looking for growth capital.

2. The AmLaw 100 will become the AmLaw 25. There will be a continuing flight to the top-paying firms which are, essentially, their own brand names. They will continue to command premium fees using hourly rates, because clients are willing to pay for the brand. All other firms will shrink in size and billings due to competition from other industries and other professions.

3. Technology will continue to strive toward the "Holy Grail" of being able to replace human analysis with algorithmic analysis. Humans will not be replaced entirely, but the specialized tasks they once performed as a means of obtaining wisdom will be technology-driven. As a result, lawyers will be forced to provide added value through analysis and strategic thinking, not just application

of the law to the facts or understanding every single document in a case. The traditional model depends on the erasure of institutional knowledge and re-creation to support the revenue base. Everyone at the large firms where I worked would lament that we didn't have a briefs library, but no one did anything, because by re-creating briefs, we made more money. With the rise of Google as a search engine and a means of collecting enterprise knowledge, it will not be long before Lexis and Westlaw face competition from Google, and they'll make this legal knowledge accessible to everyone. We had stand-alone terminals when I graduated in 1985. But today I can find most of what I need online, not on Westlaw. The keys to that knowledge kingdom have opened up. Regular people can access legal knowledge. Now it's about having the talent to employ it.

4. Domestic law schools will seek strategic partnerships with business schools and other law schools across the globe. As with the legal profession generally, "brand name" law schools will continue to pretty much function as they always have, but the second-tier schools will see a significant drop in enrollment that will cause them to expand the skill sets they offer graduates. As a result, the number of schools with a physical presence will decrease while online instruction soars. Students will be offered lectures by leading lawyers and professors and will find, online, that they actually receive more individual attention than in classes.

5. "Associates" will disappear. They will be replaced by a stepped system of apprenticeships much like what has existed in the United Kingdom.

6. Businesses will continue to make rather than buy. One of the things we're looking at in industry trends is the growth of in-house counsel. A lot of clients have decided it's cheaper to make than buy. Firms are competing with this now. And in-house counsel will have to be managed better. Although the in-house function will grow because those lawyers know the business, their management might be outsourced just as businesses have outsourced other parts of the business.

7. Capital will continue to seek its highest level of return, and litigation will be a popular means of investing. Not only will investors be offered stock in law firms; the use of third-party

funders will rise to such a level that a code of ethics will be proposed.

8. Conflicts will diminish. Although this seems counterintuitive, successful law firms will reach a natural barrier to conflict-dependent growth and will begin to insist on broad, advance waivers accompanied by non-disclosure agreements. Clients will come to rely solely on such NDAs and internal walls to prevent confidences from leaking within a law firm.

9. Second-tier firms will see an increasing amount of their business go to the top 20 firms, and they will disaggregate into regional and local firms, where many started.

10. Intellectual-property litigation will become such a barrier to innovation that Congress will once again re-define key patent concepts. Suits against internet- and website-security firms will blossom.

Teresa J. Rasmussen

SENIOR VICE PRESIDENT,
GENERAL COUNSEL AND SECRETARY
THRIVENT
MINNEAPOLIS, MN

"In our legal department, I want to make sure that the lawyers and paralegals and compliance professionals know what businesses we're in, know our mission, and develop an appreciation for the whole enterprise."

Did you do anything differently during the 2008–2009 crisis?
Not really. We're a fraternal benefit society. We're similar to a mutual-insurance company. We focus on long-term planning for the benefit of our membership. So I didn't experience the expense pressure my colleagues in public companies were under. Of course, we always want to make sure we're acting in the interests of our membership, and we certainly looked at areas to see if we could streamline our processes. We help the organization from a risk-management perspective. We help them understand where we can add value.

Our organization is very risk-averse. Our challenge as corporate counsel is to help the client understand that *risk* is not a bad word and that there's good risk and bad risk. We actively manage bad risk. We also encourage our clients to explore good risk.

In our case, you had the financial crisis, and then you had what I call the Dodd-Frank frenzy. Certain provisions of Dodd-Frank could potentially limit our ability to conduct our business as a fraternal benefit society. We have an operating company at the holding-company level, and we own a federal-savings bank, which means we were an S&L holding company under the supervision of the Federal Reserve. As a bank holding company, your activities must be "closely related to banking." As a fraternal benefit society, our members engage in charitable, social, religious, educational, and patriotic activities. For example, we are the largest corporate partner with Habitat for Humanity. Thrivent Builds with Habitat has constructed 2,700 homes since 2005 through $180 million in funding and 3.5 million volunteer hours. These activities are not what the Federal Reserve would classify as "closely related to banking." We actively influenced Dodd-Frank to allow our fraternal activities and be a bank holding company. This is one way we add value.

We also proactively explored options for our federal savings bank. Ultimately, we converted a portion of our federal savings bank to a federal credit union. Again, the legal team provided the options to the business, led the negotiations with four regulatory bodies, and helped close the transaction. This resulted in Thrivent no longer being classified as an S&L holding company.

How are you thinking about pricing and value?

We have very little outside-counsel spend. I prefer subject-matter experts to be in-house so that they can give constant, timely advice in meetings. If we don't have enough volume in certain areas to support an in-house expert, then we'll go outside. For trademarks and intellectual property, we'll find a boutique firm that can become a valued partner with us. If I need a weighty legal opinion, I'm sensitive to value, but I'm more sensitive to the author of the opinion. What's their reputation among the audience I am influencing?

We're reviewing our practices and doing some investigation in managing our overall resources. Many services can supply lawyers and paralegals temporarily at an affordable price, but if I can't buy talent outside, I have to grow that talent from within. We're an IRC 501(c)(8) fraternal organization. There's a few of us out there, but I can really only grow that talent from within. The lawyer who wrote the treatise on 501(c)(8)s works at Thrivent.

How do you manage training?

In the fraternal space, we provide organization and training. For most of the people we employ, this business is new for them. We will have lunch-and-learns. In our legal department, I want to make sure that the lawyers and paralegals and compliance professionals know what businesses we're in, know our mission, and develop an appreciation for the whole enterprise. My investment lawyers—we have a rather large investment portfolio—communicate with the corporate lawyers on a daily basis, discussing issues and transactions and sharing information.

Is the role of the general counsel becoming more active?

Generally, yes. I think there are different philosophies. I had two excellent role models in my career. I spent fifteen years at American Express working with Louise Parent, who is still the general counsel at American Express. And John Junek, who was my boss at what is now Ameriprise, was also a great role model.

Everybody has a different philosophy about the general-counsel office, and in my case, when I arrived at Thrivent, the organization had just gone through a merger of equals. My predecessor, through right-sizing or downsizing, selected very talented lawyers, but they weren't steeped in the subject matter of our regulated businesses. In the previous legal-department culture, they could wait for the phone to ring, and the first reaction to the client's question would be, "No, you can't do that." I coined the phrase that I wanted to transform us from the Department of No to the Department of Know. We should be providing value and helping the client succeed. I brought in experienced lawyers, and in the process of the last seven years, we have developed deep subject-matter expertise. We are also grooming junior lawyers to give them more responsibility and prepare them as future leaders.

You have to surround yourself with good people. I have responsibilities for a lot of people: lawyers, paralegals, compliance professionals, business-risk-management auditors, communications and Lutheran relationship professionals. We have a lot going on: life, health insurance and annuities, investment advisors, broker/dealers, private equity funds, a bank, a captive sales force of 2,500, and 1,300 chapters, all with a tax-exempt organization. We share common issues with other regulated industries but have many unique issues as well. An example of our uniqueness is our Lutheran common bond. This means we spend time with Lutheran organizations and congregations, because it's where we find our members.

How do you use technology to communicate internally?

We are a relatively small department. We use video conferencing between the two locations to stay in touch.

What legal trends have you taken advantage of within the organization?

When people become members in our organization, they agree to our dispute-resolution process, which is a wonderful thing. Our lawyers, who have worked in litigation, love this program. Any member complaint is forwarded to our member-relations compliance unit. They gather information regarding the member's complaint. We assemble an internal panel of experts who review the complaint and then render a decision. If the decision is not in favor of the member, the member can request mediation with an external party. If that's not in favor of the member, they can go to a binding arbitration process. We pay for everything. Some of our members hated this process in the beginning, but now I can't think of a member in the past seven years who hasn't been happy by the end of the process. It costs them nothing, they feel they've been heard, and they get an explanation. We, by the way, do see decisions in favor of our members in all three stages of the process. We actively resolve our members' complaints. It's very effective.

What trends do you see in the industry?

We're following different areas. Security and privacy are always active. From a regulatory standpoint, we're always sensitive to emerging sales-practice issues and new rules.

I've talked with Marianne Short, former managing partner at Dorsey Whitney, about emerging trends in the legal market. One of the trends is about finding ways to use junior lawyers better. How do they get good legal training while the client gets something of value? How do you come together and get a win-win in that partnership? It's beneficial for us to delegate responsibility to someone, and we get something of value to help a lawyer develop. In the old days, corporate clients were okay with paying for junior associates, but there's less of that willingness now. Clients are more sensitive to getting value from every lawyer involved. We've experimented with "seconding" junior lawyers on projects.

What do you see happening in the industry in the near future?

I see everyone struggling with new technology. It's not about figuring out how to use it. It's about trying to understand the legal implications of it. Our regulators struggle with this as well. In our regulatory environment, we have to keep email. Think about this transition from documents as typed hardcopies to all forms of electronic communications, including email, video, everything. We conduct live meetings using videoconferencing, and there is the presumption that this qualifies as the type of communication we have to keep. We struggle with this notion of keeping meeting minutes versus saving video of the actual meeting. I don't know if our document-retention standards are getting out of hand.

William D. Henderson

Professor of Law and Val Nolan Faculty Fellow
Director, Center on the Global Legal Profession
Maurer School of Law, Indiana University

"All firms and most lawyers in corporate legal services are cowed by brands, and this makes them risk averse. This opens the field for true innovators in LPOs. They start at a lower level and work their way up."

Are law firms waiting for things to get better, or are they changing on their own right now?
From the perspective of looking at industry-level data, I think you'll find a striking pattern. If you look at law-office employment according to U.S. Census numbers, you'll see that law employment has been flat since 2004. There are 1.1 million people who get their W2s from law firms. This does not include partners, but it does include associates, contract partners, and of-counsel. Between 2004 and 2009, that sector lost 26,000 jobs. That includes some paralegals and some lawyers. In other words, we weren't in a recession in 2004, and yet employment numbers were already slowing. The flat-lining of legal employment started years before Lehman Brothers in the fall 2008.

So, in 2004, the number of legal jobs flat-lines. There was no growth in this sector, like there was in last five to six decades. What's the interpretation? If people think the changes are driven by this recession, they are fooling themselves. The data is based on FICA returns. There is no mystery to this. The problems in the legal industry are not cyclical. The changes are structural.

Another census category to look at is All Other Legal Services, which includes temporary-employment agencies, domestic legal-process outsourcers, etc. That sector has grown like gangbusters. It used to be about 9,000 people, but now it's over 20,000. That sector has added 6,000 jobs since 2004. Yes, it's only 6,000 new jobs versus the loss of 26,000 in law offices, but this is the way disruptive technologies manifest themselves. LPOs figure out a way to take low-hanging fruit and scale up operations to move up the value chain.

Law firms have not been growing like they used to in past decades. This creates huge problems for traditional law firms. You have young energetic associates who want to rise up the ladder, but they're bumping into older partners reluctant to retire. So there are not enough openings to reward associates who have worked hard. When associates join as partners, they dilute the partnership money to split. So a firm has to get honest and make sure it doesn't have incentives that work against generations. The traditional partner/associate paradigm presumes constant growth. Today, a firm has to be realistic about work. It has to create a new structure that is not dependent on a presumption of constant, steady growth.

People are seizing the opportunities created by the inefficiencies of the billable hour. Firms want to sell time, but clients want to buy value. Basing your model on delivering value requires lawyers to rework their operations and do more with less. Law firms can't base their business models on raising hourly rates every year. Think of it in terms of this analogy. In the old days, the horse-and-buggy companies were *not* in the horse-and-buggy business. They were in the *transportation* business. The companies that didn't understand that crucial difference went out of business completely. Today, lawyers have to realize they are not in the business of selling *time*. They are in the business of selling *solutions*.

This is a crucial difference, and the lawyers who don't understand this will go out of business.

The romantic myth of the lawyer is still seductive, though. Lawyers wear nice suits. They work in wood-paneled courtrooms. They are attractive people who enjoy cocktails after work. Who doesn't want to be affluent and attractive and not have to do manual labor? For a long time, the myth had some basis in reality. Pursuing a career in the law was like getting on an escalator. You worked hard in college, you went to a decent law school, you graduated, and you joined a law firm. Without much thought, you could have a prosperous life for yourself. You were more or less guaranteed to join the ranks of the middle class to upper-middle class. Law was a growth business. Sophisticated clients always needed more lawyers to handle new regulations and complex finance issues and more.

The real story today, however, is very different. The business world is more competitive. Clients can't afford to pay on the basis of hours and materials. We are in a time when we're thinking about law from an engineering perspective. We need to move on this continuum. The world wants us to go in this direction. Clients want predictability and standardization.

How do you transition to a new model?

Brands are powerful and vivid. People have a hard time disentangling substance from brand reputation. Fred Bartlit realized this. He wanted to build a better model that better served his clients and used an alternative-fee model in the early Nineties. But lots of people have a hard time imagining the future. There is no guarantee of achieving success. You have to build a new brand. You can't rely on an existing brand. This is difficult to do. Basically, the legal media has a lot to do with building a brand. It's going to take time.

Here's an example. Joe Flom and Marty Lipton did hostile-takeover work in late Sixties and Seventies. They were Jewish, so they were never going to be successful with white-shoe law firms. They went out on their own. The very first issue of *American Lawyer* featured pictures of Flom and Lipton and an article in which they talked about how much money they were making. The new legal press flipped the image, and hostile-takeover work shifted from being regarded as unseemly work to being seen as exciting, profitable work. It was ingenious on Joe Flom's part, but the image flipped in part because the legal press made it so.

People stepping out today have substance on their side but no protection of a hefty brand. So there is some reluctance for clients to switch away from the big firms. If I'm a GC, I have a choice: I can hire some new boutique with firm refugees for value, or I can hire a standard law firm with an established reputation. If I hired the value firm and the matter blows up, then I might be blamed because I hired an off-brand law firm. If I hired a big-name firm, I can't be second-guessed.

So these off-brand folks have to start lower on the value chain. They can't do high-profile work, and they have to learn about branding and how to build a brand that's distinctive. All firms and most lawyers in corporate legal services are cowed by brands, and this makes them risk averse. This opens the field for true innovators in LPOs. They start at a lower level and work their way up.

Will there be new ways for lawyers to practice? In other words, will their roles change?

I published an article on the three generations of lawyers: the generalist, the specialist, and the project manager. The historical development gives you an analytical frame of supply and demand, and the narrative makes sense and holds together. The generalist has evolved into the specialist. Today, we have overpriced specialists. What's next is evolving into the role of the project manager.

Unlike existing partners and legal specialists, who don't want to change, legal entrepreneurs and young people who are entering a cold marketplace have the advantage of not being invested in the old ways. They are free to start a new business from scratch, and they're more likely to do it. Traditional employers are giving them the cold shoulder, and now they're more than happy to compete with them and take them down.

We're at the beginning of a whole new era of unpacking conventions. It's not that certain things are not valuable. The law firm's brand is valuable, but clients aren't willing to overpay for the brand anymore. They want to pay what the brand is worth. In general, people tend to pay too much attention to obvious indicators, like a brand. If you don't have all the information you want, you rely on other proxy indicators that are easily available. People make judgments using an availability heuristic: you base too much of your judgment on information that's easily available, whether or not it's relevant. There is plenty of room for error and inaccuracy here. So that's what causes a brand to be overvalued and creates opportunities for new entrants. There's a gap between perceived value and actual value. New entrants can take advantage of that gap in value. New entrants can sell the same quality of service for a corrected price that more accurately reflects actual value.

Are you surprised at the pace of change in the industry?

I'm surprised at the slow change. As a general rule, people tend to overestimate the changes that will happen in five years and underestimate the changes that will happen in ten years. This is complicated stuff. In most industries, you're trying to improve the lots of three groups: owners, workers, and customers. In the legal industry, we are trying to do the same thing, to devise a system in which we make three groups better off: partners, lawyers, and clients. But right now, no model can be put neatly in place where all three are made better off. Until we can find a new sustainable model, we're going to grope in the dark.

Young lawyers need to be trained, but they also need to be respected. The younger lawyers are the ones who tend to be innovative. We have to listen to what they're coming up with, because right now there's no easy transitional phase to move us from the associate/partner model to one that doesn't necessarily grow but still makes everyone better off. If you're a partner who has been working for decades, you're invested in the current model until you retire. You don't want to switch. The market may force you to make some changes, but the changes are risky, too. The transitional phase is foggy, because you don't know where you're going. You don't know exactly what model you're heading toward. I don't see any firm that has struck gold with a new model.

So will the industry be balkanized for a while, containing a plurality of different models?

Well, LPOs do pretty well. You can start with discovery, and you can move to labor and employment law and trusts and estates, etc. You can move up to places where legal process is amenable. And here you're picking off low-level legal work. If you bundle these together and apply process to it or include a counseling package, you can make serious money, and the people who are going to do it are those who have invested in process. Seyfarth Shaw has invested heavily in Six Sigma. They have a chance. They might turn the corner and represent the next model. There's going to be a heck of a lot of change to manage. Law firms can be huge organizations, and the big ones have been successful for thirty or forty years under a different paradigm, run by partners who still have a few years left at the top. This is where I think people have a hard time getting their head around why the elite firms can't just change on a dime and adopt a new biz model. It's the same reason GM was susceptible to Toyota. In 1970s, Toyota came to the market with rusting little cars, and now Lexus is a stronger brand than Cadillac. The law-firm leaders of today can't imagine this happening to them, but it can.

Can change be driven by proactive GCs who know exactly how to tell firms to change?

Whoever writes the check controls the outcome. But it takes a lot of thought. It's difficult to resolve how you're going to achieve the goals of quality, cost and timeliness. I've observed that the most innovative GCs do not have law backgrounds, like Mark Chandler and one of his lieutenants, Steve Harmon. One of the GCs at Cook Medical never worked in a law firm, and they put their outside counsel on flat fees.

This is about optimization and taking existing work and doing it in a more fundamental way. You need to leverage existing technology, reform workplace operation, and boost collaboration. Society needs more lawyers very badly. There is a great deal of work that lawyers need to do. I've looked at these changes for a long time. I've talked to so many lawyers, and I've tried to come up with a theory that takes account of all the data points and the experiences of all the people I've talked to. And I have to say I'm worried about what might be called a fluid transition to something else. There may be creative destruction that goes on. No one likes to see firms struggle and go out of business. But that will happen. The flip side is there will be lots of opportunity.

What can law schools do better today to prepare new attorneys to survive in this transitional period in the industry?

I can tell you what I'm doing. I see this as a great time of opportunity for legal educators. We've created a law school at Maurer where we've invested time and energy in coursework that develops teamwork, collaboration, listening skills, networking, personality assessments, presentation skills, and communication skills. I want my students to fare better in terms of selling themselves.

We're rapidly moving to a selection model for legal services that looks at past performance. If you don't understand how you're being evaluated for jobs, you'll be caught flat-footed. Students have to demonstrate performance in the past to get jobs in the future. You have to do this in law school. You have to find your blind spots in law school and correct them. You have to find out what motivates you besides money and prestige. You have to get around bad fits with employers.

Employers who rely on performance metrics to evaluate lawyers are moving beyond traditional criteria, like where you went to law school, and are looking for people who will be successful in collaborative environments that are focused on generating value. When you have a new way of doing things, you need a new way to evaluate talent.

Allison Karnoff

WEST BLOOMFIELD, MI
CHICAGO, IL

"All students need to pay more attention to how they're going to repay their loans. And they need to be careful about the first jobs they take. In this market, everyone is told to take whatever job they can get. That has consequences, because the first thing recruiters ask is how much you currently make. If you start low, you stay low."

Part I: March 2011

What's your status?

I graduated from the University of Wisconsin law school in the spring of 2010. I am admitted to the bar in Wisconsin due to bar privilege, I passed the bar in Illinois, and I am waiting to hear if I passed the bar in Michigan. I live in my parent's house in West Bloomfield, Michigan, to save money. I'm unemployed.

I am an unpaid judicial intern for the chief justice of the federal district court in Detroit. Otherwise, I'm ten months out after graduation, and I still haven't made a penny, not one in 2011. My peers are jumping into non-legal positions. I went into law school wanting to practice. I'm holding out and seeing what happens. I was lucky to get the internship with the judge. I'm waiting for the right moment. I don't want to move for a part-time job. I really want to practice in Chicago, but I can't finance a move there without the right job.

I keep my spirits up, because I know unemployment has nothing to do with me. I worked for a midsize firm as a 2L, but they couldn't hire me for financial reasons. We had a great relationship. They even put it in writing. The president of the firm wrote that "under any other circumstances, we would have hired Allison." So that's been helpful for my state of mind, knowing that I have recommendations and good references. I had the occasion to meet the president of a law firm in Minneapolis. I met him at a pool near my parents' condo in Florida. He said lawyers were working as paralegals now.

What was the feel like in law school among you and your peers as you were getting close to graduating? Were you apprehensive?

I was in the class of 2010. Everything fell out from under of us before we saw the light at the end of the tunnel, but we were too close to the end to leave. I've been so impressed with my peers who've taken the change in circumstance and realized they can't practice now, so they're taking whatever jobs they can to be in the best position to build up experience for when the time comes. I think schools will go more toward pushing specialization, but when I was there, the more common thing was you got the job through your summer-associate position, not based on what course work you took during law school. One of my friends specialized in an area, and she couldn't find a job in a law firm. She wanted labor law, and so she went to work for a union as a union rep. I know someone who was sixth in his class at Wisconsin, and he's not employed in law either. He's working in the field but not as a lawyer. Someone like him should have a job. The legal industry may lose people forever, as they enter jobs outside the law.

What made you want to go to law school?

I was pursuing a journalism degree as an undergrad at Michigan State University, but I fell out of love with it and started considering law school. Around the same time, the Honors College I was a part of sent out an email from a local attorney looking to hire a paralegal. I responded and got the job, starting at the end of my sophomore year. He was looking for someone to take on a lot of responsibility. He promised to provide a good recommendation for law school, but he couldn't pay well. So he hired students for two years as they got experience, trained each other, and left. I went in at 19 years old, and within five months, I was experienced in immigration law. I worked directly with clients, researched and applied the law.

The gentleman I worked for died fifteen months after I joined the firm, and he was the sole practitioner. While my boss's heath declined, he discussed a merger with another law firm in our building. It was the summer before my senior year of college, and I wondered if I should have a fun year or stay at this place and deal with the transition. Then, within two weeks of the merger, the gentleman died. In the months preceding the merger, I kept the practice running to make sure it survived. Some staff left. There were five people, but then there were just me and one other paralegal, who managed all the files and worked on everything from finances to inventory. We cut our own checks, coordinated with clients, dealt with paperwork, and kept the whole firm afloat. Ultimately, we notified the clients of the merger and the death in the same correspondence. In response to our letter, I got three phone calls from clients saying they'd be okay as long as I was still there. So I felt like law was something I was supposed to do. I had to deal with the ethical barrier between acting as a paralegal and a lawyer on a daily basis, so I realized I couldn't see myself staying a paralegal. I wanted to handle it all and be a lawyer. So law school was the destination.

I was doing family-immigration law, and the negative cases would follow me home at night, lying in bed thinking about the clients. I called it bad-news law. It took a personal toll. I still think about clients' cases that were unfinished when I left the firm upon graduation. I worked closely with one client and bonded over her emotional Violence Against Women Act filing. She and I still email each other. The experience shaped the kind of lawyer I can be.

How did you like law school?

Wisconsin teaches law in action, so they try to push how things are done in practice. Even our more substantive courses are a little more practice-oriented. I did clinical work through school for three semesters. I was talking to clients, writing letters, doing motions. Other students did *pro bono* projects. I anticipate those clinical programs will grow, and more firms will take on second-year free clerks, to get more free work. One thing about this down market is maybe schools will better prepare you for practice.

I've been a student my whole life, and I didn't realize how much of your time in law school was spent trying to get a job. I didn't specialize. I took classes that interested me and were practical, making myself a diverse candidate: pre-trial advocacy, trial advocacy, negotiations, oral communication, advanced legal writing. I interned with the Wisconsin Supreme Court. I tried to show that I didn't spend three years in class memorizing notes. And I'm saying in my letters to firms that I have legal experience, and I've spent three years working on practical legal skills. And so far, this hasn't worked for me. It hasn't been enough. The market has changed, but hiring decision-making hasn't. It's going to take a while for hiring decision-making to change and catch up.

What was career placement like in your law school?

There are full- and part-time staff, at least four or five people there at Wisconsin. Some students took more advantage than I did during law school. We have an online job board. I keep in email contact with one person in the office, and he keeps a lookout for anything that crosses his desk that might fit me.

What kind of interview process did you go through on campus?

I got my summer-associate position through on-campus interviewing. I got a summer position at the only Michigan firm that came to Wisconsin, a midsized Lansing-based firm with various satellite offices, including one near my hometown. I was familiar with and admired the firm from my time as a paralegal. I essentially got a callback on the spot. I wanted to work in Chicago, but I knew I should keep my options open. Once I received rejection letters from all my Chicago firms, I wished and hoped the Michigan firm would hire me. Thankfully, they did, and I worked at the office 12 minutes away from my parents' house.

You were in the start of your 2L year during the crash in the fall of 2008. What was going on for you at that time?
The market fell out during my interview period. All my interviews were scheduled for September of 2008. I wanted to work in Chicago at a mid-sized firm. I wasn't at the top of my class, and I didn't go to one of the top law schools, so I was ultimately locked out of Chicago. My focus on mid-sized firms led to callbacks at firms intending to have summer classes with between 1–10 students. Once hiring decisions were made, many of the firms had reduced the size of their summer-associate class. I was terrified that I wouldn't get any position, and I knew I was very lucky when I got my position in Michigan. During my 3L year, the career-placement office felt as out of place and lost as we students felt. They were trying everything they could to figure out this market. Before the crash, a recruiting company said the most important thing a law grad could do was to choose your first law job carefully in an area you really liked, because you could get pigeon-holed in that substantive field. A year later, after the crash, the recruiters and advisors were shouting to take any job you can get!

Do you think your experience at the small firm will help you get a job?
I want to say my experience at the immigration firm inspired me to start my own practice, but honestly, I have to say that working at a very small firm had the opposite effect on me. It made me want to run as far away as possible. Before law school, I was a 20-year-old office manager and a paralegal, and the administrative side took away a lot from doing actual law-related work. During law school, as a summer associate, I was at a hundred-lawyer firm: they had a librarian and an accounting department. I liked that better. Now, though, a small firm may appreciate that I had that past small-firm experience.

What is your debt like?

I went to an out-of-state law school completely on loans. It was a family thing where, originally, my parents were going to help me pay for loans. Unfortunately, the market has eliminated that possibility. At the time, my parents stressed that money should have no bearing on my decision-making: that I should make choices based upon what school felt right and what school would lead me toward my goal of working in Chicago. I didn't think enough about it. Actually, I probably didn't think of the ramifications of the debt at all. I didn't apply to in-state law schools where I knew I could get full scholarships, and I turned down large scholarships from multiple lower-ranked schools. There were a lot of pros and cons going from undergrad to law school. I'd told myself I'd be fine with loans, but if you don't graduate right into a job, then your loans just grow. I did a little calculation. All my loans total $150,774. I don't know what the rate was when I graduated, but by October 2010, before my six-month deferment ended, I already had $8,000 in interest. On November 16, six months out, that was when interest capitalized if I didn't pay off the interest, and my loan base jumped to $165,808. Now, because I'm unemployed and have to continue deferments, it's going to capitalize again. Today it would add another $7,000. I think it capitalizes again at the end of May. So my debt increased over $14,000 because I was unemployed and using deferments which capitalize interest. That's a $22,000 difference from the start of the deferment at graduation. While I'm not forced to make payments now with money I don't have, my loan debt keeps growing as I sit here and defer.

How does this affect what kind of job you can accept?

Recently, I did a hypothetical budget comparison between Chicago and Michigan. I need $40,000 a year in Chicago, not including car insurance, clothing, toiletries, etc. It's just rent and loans. I'll be paying $1,100 to $1,300 a month in loans. In Michigan, I need only $25,000 a year. But even the best job in Michigan doesn't look good to Chicago firms, and if I want to get to Chicago, I have to think about that.

I'm aware of how much I would've been able to make if I'd just gotten an average marketing job after undergrad. I could've moved to Chicago and made what I need to make now, but now I have $170,000 of debt. I think law students need a primer on this. My family and I didn't think about it. Even looking back, I imagine that, had I known, I still would've said, "This won't happen to me. I won't be unemployed. I'm a great candidate." That's a common mentality. Maybe people should work for four to five years after undergrad and before law school to have a financial cushion. Now my loans dictate all my decisions.

I tell my parents the problem is being overeducated. I can't forget that if I go in at a low pay grade, I may never catch up to my peers. If I start doing a non-law or non-lawyer job, I may be stuck, with no one wanting to train me later on down the road. It's an interesting personal battle.

How are you looking for jobs?

I have my first interview in Chicago coming up. So because I have this interview, I worked out my budget. I know firms want to pay $40,000 and not give benefits. I know through Craigslist some firms only accept applicants who indicate a salary. My parents run their own company, and I wrote their Craigslist ad when they were looking to hire someone, and even I wrote down the salary indication. So I understand both sides. But committing to a lowball salary obviously screws the applicant. I want to know how to negotiate with a firm. So I did the reasonable budget calculations. This way I know what salary I can accept and live on.

So law firms are using Craigslist to hire law graduates?

I saw a Craigslist ad for paralegals from a law firm that wanted "attorneys willing to work for paralegal pay."

A funny thing happened when I worked for the sole practitioner before I went to law school. We got an unsolicited application from the number-one student in his graduating class at Thomas M. Cooley Law School. That stuck in my head, because the other paralegal and I were applying for law school, and here's this number-one guy applying to be right where we were at that point. Competition is so much harder today. I've been unemployed long enough now to be competing with this summer's associates, and then I'll be competing with the next graduating class!

Why do you want to work in Chicago so badly?

It's just always what I wanted to do. I always wanted to go. My parents took me there all the time. Chicago was the big city. I always had friends there, and I was always visiting. Now in this market, I have to ask myself, "Do I want to be taken advantage of, or do I want to be employed?"

Part II: January 2012

A lot has changed for you in the nine months since we last spoke. You have a job in Chicago.

Yes. I live and work on Michigan Avenue in downtown Chicago. I had to go an hour and a half away for court this morning. My funny story is I got the job at the end of April last year, and they gave me nine days to move to Chicago and start. I graduated from law school on May 14, 2010, and I started my first job one year later on May 9, 2011. I sent my careers services an email advising them of my new position, mocking that I qualified for the "employed after 12 months" with only five days to spare.

How did you get your job?

My job was the first interview I was offered, the one we spoke about while I was unemployed. I ultimately interviewed with two firms on one trip to Chicago. The second firm offered me the job first. It was an asbestos-litigation firm, and they offered me $41,000 a year and seemed to think this was a very high salary. I turned down the job before hearing back from the initial firm. My firm offered me $60,000 with no moving benefits and no signing bonus. That's the economy. They don't need to do those things. My firm has ten lawyers and represents equipment lessors and finance institutions. We do commercial litigation, and creditor-side bankruptcy. My firm liked that I had the multiple-state licenses. With my addition, our firm can represent matters in Wisconsin and Michigan, potentially without the necessity of local counsel. I sobbed all night after receiving the $60,000 job offer. I wanted to be excited for myself and proud, but I was terrified about the low income with my debt load. In spite of that, I knew I was lucky. I found my job in a way they say you shouldn't. They say only a limited number of people find jobs on job boards, but I found mine that way, although it still took a year.

The main theme of your story, though, is persistence. You didn't give up.

I got very lucky because Chicago lawyers were telling me for months to give up on Chicago if I didn't live there. I was in Detroit, and I had no Chicago connections. So then I applied for reciprocity on the Chicago-Kent Law School job board, and on the first day I had access to it, I applied to the position which turned into my job. The Chicago-Kent connection is pretty ironic, because I had been accepted there but had turned it down to go to Wisconsin, often wondering post-grad if I made the right decision, since I wanted to end up in Chicago!

How do you like your job?

I'm still here. We do commercial litigation, and, accordingly, I do a lot of post-judgment collections. I didn't really understand that I would be doing collections when I interviewed, but I am gaining a lot of experience litigating in state and federal courts. I still stand by them, because I got what I wanted: a full-time law job in downtown Chicago.

How are you managing your debt?

Over the year I was unemployed, my loans capitalized by $25,000. I had put my loans on deferment for unemployment, and when I started my new job, I called my loan servicer to determine which repayment plan would require the lowest monthly payment so I could get on my feet and build some semblance of a savings account. I actually had the loan servicer giggling on the phone when we determined that income-based repayment would be the best for me: the payments are based on 2010 income, and since mine was non-existent, my monthly payment is set at $0. In May, I will start having a monthly amount due, based upon my 2011 earnings. They're not slamming the full amount on me. I'd never be able to do it.

What advice would you give today to recent law graduates?

All students need to pay more attention to how they're going to repay their loans. And they need to be careful about the first jobs they take. The salary level you accept keeps you down as you hunt for new positions. In this market, everyone is told to take whatever job they can get. This is risky, because if I hadn't had the potential for the $60,000 job, I would've felt pressured to take the $41,000 job. That has consequences, because the first thing recruiters ask is how much you currently make. So if you start low, you stay low. It's tough if you take the first lowball offer out of desperation. You get pegged at that level. I didn't realize that's the number-one question recruiters ask.

Do you think your practical experience helped you in any way?
A couple things helped. I used my time to pass the bars in Illinois and Michigan to add to my Wisconsin admission. My firm here in Chicago has me using my Wisconsin bar. So if we have cases in Milwaukee, I can handle those cases. That's an advantage.

Another thing that's changed is that firms are more willing to look at individuals with a year of experience somewhere else. In this market, you feel like you're under a take-any-job-you-can-get mindset, but firms are looking at a broader scope of candidates. A friend of mine was fired, and within days, he had three interviews. Experience counts for a lot. Firms like not paying to train you. I also have more hands-on experience, and I'm willing to work for a lower salary because I needed the job and I wanted to work in Chicago. Now that's for small and medium firms. If you're trying to break into a big firm in this market, you need more than just general experience. You need particularized skills, because the big firm can find another candidate with work experience for cheaper than they could in the past.

Are you happy with Chicago?
I intend to be a lifer here in Chicago.

Part III: June 2012

Are you still with the same firm?
Yes. My one-year anniversary was May 9, 2012. I was bumped up in salary from $60,000 to $65,000 a year.

How does your work experience compare with the experiences of people you know?
I read that a Boston law firm posted an opening for a $10,000/year associate position on a job board and had 32 applicants.

[See: "More Than 50 Would-Be Associates Have Now Applied for $10,000-a-Year Boston Law Firm Job," Martha Neil, *ABAJournal.com*, June 11, 2012.]

And just yesterday, I saw on the Chicago Daily Law Bulletin a posting for a Chicago attorney with three years of experience, and the pay was $45,000. These salaries are lower than the salaries for paralegal jobs. Why go to law school? I know that the class of 2011 had the worst placement in history.

[See, at end of this interview, an excerpt from "Law School Grads Face Worst Job Market Yet—Less Than Half Find Jobs in Private Practice," NALP, June 7, 2012.]

Are you applying for other jobs?

I have to if I want more money or to change fields. My firm generally has had more junior associates than mid- or senior-level associates, so I am unsure about my long-term potential. I'm applying to jobs all the time, but the ones who call me back are similarly small firms offering lower salaries. In looking at other positions, I have to wonder what's better than where I am right now. I manage my own cases, and I know what I have to do and the trajectory of the cases for the next year. It would be nice to have more variety and some unknowns in my future, for better or worse. Certainly, parts of my job are great. I'm getting good experience in state and federal courts, but I don't enjoy the high volume of commercial-collection matters. I like the contested cases and doing discovery, and all that experience is enjoyable and worthwhile for my career.

How is your loan situation?

I looked up my loan principle, and it is $176,000. I'm accruing $1,000 a month in interest, which is outrageous. I already have $7,000 in accrued interest. I just learned that if you earn enough to get out of the income-based repayment plan, then that interest will capitalize. I took out $150,000 to pay for law school, and when I am able finally to start paying the loan back, I could be nearing a loan debt of $200,000. I've been paying $0 per month on the income-based repayment plan, because I didn't have earnings in 2010. This year, I'll be paying based on 2011, and I'll be paying less than $300 per month with interest continuing to accrue.

I feel like I'm as naïve living with these loans as I was as a 1L. I guess this is something I'm going to be dealing with for a long time. I don't know how to make it better.

I have heard that parents are taking out home-equity loans at 3% and paying off their children's law-school loans, which are fixed between 6% and 8%. Then the law grads pay off their parents' loans at the significantly reduced rate. The high fixed rates on the student loans is very unfortunate. I know my various loans are fixed between 6% and 8.5%, the bulk of them at the higher level.

Are you happy that you live and work in Chicago?

As much as my journey has not been what I wanted it to be, I still want to be in Chicago. While my job is low paying, it does not demand as much of my time as a high-paying job likely would. I am lucky to have free time to enjoy the city. If I were home in Michigan, I may not feel as happy about it. But here I have lots of things to do after work. I live right downtown.

Are you networking with people?

You never know who knows who and what firm is hiring. I try to stay in contact with previous recruiters and other attorneys, because you never know. A lot of times with networking, it's the luck of timing. I think things are getting better, but firms are settling into the expectation that they can get great people for much less money.

So now law grads aren't just competing against each other. They're competing directly against experienced lateral hires who are ready to work for lower salaries.

New and experienced lawyers are competing, but firms are also looking for the cheapest option.

My friend interviewed with a small firm in 2009 as a recent graduate. He didn't get the job, but a couple weeks ago, he applied to a blind ad on the ChicagoDaily Job Bulletin. It turned out to be that same firm that rejected him in 2009. The firm told him they didn't hire him in 2009 because they were able to hire a third-year lateral from Jones Day.

Part IV: February 2013

Any change in your status?

Nothing has changed in my status, except that my loan debt has grown to over $188,000.

Are you learning anything new about the business of practicing law?

There are now three associates who joined the firm substantially later than me, so I am in a position in which I have other attorneys coming to me for direction—be it substantive, procedural, or based on firm practice. So I have gained an appreciation for how much I truly have learned over the last (almost) two years of practice. I am also getting more varied cases, with a lot of the routine cases going to the more junior associates, so that increases my job satisfaction. I'm looking ahead and hoping for another raise when I hit my two-year anniversary, though I know it will all be sunk into my loans (in a fit of frustration, I sent $3,000 in last Thursday).

Of course, everything comes full circle. My legal assistant is about to start an LSAT-prep course, and I am doing everything I can think of to respectfully suggest that she seriously consider the investment and the opportunity cost. The years spent in school and early practice are years that our peers are gaining experience in other fields. Just a few years out, I already know one attorney who is leaving the practice, and a few more who have given themselves one to two more years before they get out. Had we begun in another industry all those years ago, we might have been, by now, established and debt-free.

All in all, I love Chicago. I am lucky to have a job, but the debt is incapacitating. Recently, I read an article about how Millennials are likely to be forced to make life decisions (like delaying marriage and forgoing children) based upon their student debt. I'm a prime example.

* **Excerpt from "Law School Grads Face Worst Job Market Yet—Less Than Half Find Jobs in Private Practice," NALP, June 7, 2012:**

According to Selected Findings from the Employment Report and Salary Survey for the Class of 2011 released today by NALP, the overall employment rate for new law school graduates is, at 85.6%, the lowest it has been since 1994, when the rate stood at 84.7%. In addition to an overall employment rate that fell two percentage points from that for the previous class, and that has dropped each year since 2008, the Class of 2011 employment figures reveal a job market with many underlying structural weaknesses. The employment profile for this class also marks a continued interruption of employment patterns for new law school graduates that had, prior to 2010, been undisturbed for decades.

The NALP Employment Report and Salary Survey for the Class of 2011 measures the employment rate of graduates as of February 15, 2012, or nine months after a typical May graduation. Analyses of these data reveal an employment rate that has fallen more than six percentage points since reaching a 23-year high of 91.9% in 2007 and marks the lowest employment rate since the aftermath of the last significant recession to affect the U.S. legal economy. The Class of 1994 was the last class with an employment rate lower than that for the Class of 2011, and since 1985 there have only been three classes with an overall employment rate below 85.6%. All of those occurred in the aftermath of the 1990–1991 recession: 83.5% for 1992, 83.4% for 1993, and 84.7% for 1994.

See: *Jobs & JD's: Employment and Salaries of New Law School Graduates—Class of 2011*

Carrie Hightman

EXECUTIVE VICE PRESIDENT &
CHIEF LEGAL OFFICER
NiSource
MERRILLVILLE, IN

"One of the things that's important to me is making sure we get women and minorities in at lower levels as associates at our outside firms. If they don't get training and get in the pipeline, how do they move up and ultimately get billing credit? How do they advance in their careers?"

How long have you been at NiSource?
I've been here five years as of December 2012. I came from AT&T. I was president of AT&T's Illinois operations.

How did you make the move?
I'd never been in the role of general counsel before. I'd always done regulated industries: electric, water, etc. This was a new opportunity that fit.

How was that transition?

As a senior executive at a major corporation—running the supply chain, IT, HR, or the legal department, for example—you're managing people and issues. My last role at AT&T prepared me for what I do now. I don't really practice law. I manage and strategize and am a partner with my colleagues.

Was it a big deal to take over as GC?

There were no sacred cows, and I had free reign. I did a complete assessment of the department and outside counsel, and I significantly overhauled the legal department and created a preferred-provider program. A lot of what we're talking about now with pricing and value, I began to address five years ago.

How do you deal with pricing?

One of my biggest frustrations is that you can't completely jettison the billable hour. There's no alternative-fee arrangement I know that is completely divorced from cost per hour. We started looking for discounts five years ago, and now we're looking at fixed fees, blended rates, risk collars, and fee caps. We have preferred providers. We view them as partners. We put this in place three years ago. We've only replaced a couple of them. We are partners working together to come up with good, creative solutions to help NiSource meet its business goals.

Did you do anything differently during the start of the recession?

We had already put preferred providers in place, and we were able to maintain discounts. We even added a bankruptcy specialist to address bankruptcies by our customers and vendors. But it has to be fair for both sides. At the beginning of the program, I had a lot of bargaining power, but you can't abuse it.

How are you as a GC staying involved with larger industry issues?

I'm involved with industry legal groups. I'm a member of the legal committee in the trade association for electric utilities, and we meet twice a year. I'm involved in the ABA Public Utility law section. I'm also a member of the general counsel roundtable.

The more I read about alternative fees, the more I want to try them. The most current articles I've read are about clients rejecting expenses that law firms are trying to pass onto them. We already don't pay a lot of the expenses that I remember we used to pass on back when I was in private practice—for example, charges for faxing and photocopying.

One of the things that's important to me is making sure we get women and minorities in at lower levels as associates at our outside firms. If they don't get training and get in the pipeline, how do they move up and ultimately get billing credit? How do they advance in their careers?

You created a program within NiSource called "Building the Next Gen: Women in Leadership," and you held its first summit in November 2012. The purpose of the program is, as you've said, "to recruit, retain, and develop women leaders at NiSource."

The point is to develop women employees within the company. I'm the most senior woman executive at the company. I kicked this off in 2011. We invited approximately 150 women employees at NiSource to the first annual "Women in Leadership" summit in Chicago. We had great speakers on women's careers and challenges.

At the end of the summit, we asked the women what they wanted us to do next. They said we should hold a summit for the more junior women and launch a mentoring program. Since November of 2011, we rolled out an affinity group that's employee-driven, and we started a pilot mentoring program with sixteen mentors and mentees. I'm a mentor, and I'm very happy with how the program is going.

We have also held three regional meetings for the next 300 women in the organization. We used an abridged version of the November program, added speakers, and took advantage of the program content we already created, but we shortened it and tailored it for the next level of women.

The second summit was held over two days in November 2012, just before the Thanksgiving holiday. How did this summit go?

It was a great success and very well received. There was a big jump in attendance. For the first summit a year ago, we invited

155 people, and about 135 people attended. This year, we invited 190, and 180 showed up. To be invited, you have to be a manager who supervises or above. More women had been promoted in the company in the last year, and so we could invite more women. The jump in attendance was also a result of more women knowing about the program and asking for invitations to be sent to women in the company who otherwise would not be invited. We have separate regional meetings for women at junior levels in the company. All sixteen mentees from the pilot mentor program attended, no matter what level they were at, and we had some male executives and board members.

What are the components of the summit?
Last year, we had breakout sessions. This year, everyone heard every speaker. On the second day, we had two workshops everyone attended. The summit this year was more interactive and involved more networking and other activities. On the second day, we had optional networking activities for people to enjoy Chicago. Women who wanted to stay an extra half day could choose to go to the Art Institute or holiday shopping on Michigan Avenue (it was the week before Thanksgiving).

We also held an optional dinner at Kendall College, a for-profit culinary school in Chicago, and 100 women attended. We watched a demonstration about preparing holiday dishes, and then we had dinner and looked out over Chicago's skyline. We wanted to give attendees options that took advantage of the location. Our offices are located in an Indiana suburb west of Chicago, so the location was convenient for us. Last year, we packed in content. This year, we took advantage of the location and allowed for much more networking.

A key component of the summit is networking. Attendees meet speakers, some male executives, and a few board members, but most importantly, they are able to interact with each other. Some of the women have worked together for years but never met. For many of them, the summit is the first time they've been able to make personal contact. We learned at the last summit that just being able to sit face to face with a colleague is invaluable. And there is always value in meeting new people in the company. My presentations at the summits have been about—among other things—the value of networking in one's career.

How much time and planning did the summit require?
It did take a lot of time for me, and it's hard. We started planning soon after the last summit ended. I'm a perfectionist, and this is a passion I have. I want it to come out the way I want it to come out. With my professional background in Chicago, I was able to draw on my resources and network to get speakers. All the optional activities were organized by the affinity group that was created after last year's summit. The affinity group is very much membership-driven. The volunteer officers took the lead in organizing the optional activities.

What kinds of issues did the speakers address?
A professor from Cornell's business school, for example, talked about verbal and nonverbal communication differences between genders. It was fun, fascinating, and eye-opening to hear her discuss the things we don't realize we do when we communicate.

Have you received feedback from this year's attendees?
During the summit, people asked if they could volunteer to help with the regional meetings. We do have a post-meeting survey, but we haven't seen the final results yet. I expect we'll do what we did last year. We'll continue what we've started. Planning for next year is already under way.

What we do for programming for each summit, however, will change over time. We're gauging how people received different types of speakers and activities. What I've learned is that the more practical and constructive the advice, the more well received it is.

The affinity group met recently, and I asked if anyone wanted to start any new affinity groups. We're trying to figure out what people in the company are interested in. Young professionals expressed interested in forming an affinity group, possibly.

The women's program seems to be well under way. It's sustainable. It's part of our DNA. No questions have been asked about whether or not we're going to keep doing it. It's about where and when we're going to do it.

In August, you were appointed to be one of the commissioners of the ABA Commission on Women in the Profession.

The group was created back in the '80s. It's a plum assignment. As a commissioner, I appeared as a panelist at the Women in Law Leadership (WILL) in San Francisco in December. It was a two-day meeting for junior women in the law. Before I went, I invited three junior women members from my legal department to attend. I also reached out to law firms of ours, and I asked them to think about sending their women members. Two to three firms sent women to these meetings, and several women came up to me at the meeting and said they were so grateful. How nice it was to give women in our department and from our outside firms a little extra professional boost! A fellow commissioner in Women in the Profession sent a mass email about how happy she was about the success of the WILL conference, and she pointed me out, because I pushed hard to get our law firms to send women. The WILL event was something the firms wouldn't have otherwise known about. The men in charge wouldn't have thought to send anyone. Just opening your mouth and speaking your mind can make a difference.

Richard Susskind

LEGAL ADVISER, PROFESSOR, AUTHOR
RADLETT, ENGLAND

"I've watched lawyers' attitudes change and adapt over the years. Technology's time has now come for the world of law. By 2016 or 2017, for example, e-discovery and online legal services will have transformed the way litigation is handled around the world."

Most lawyers know you as the author of the book *The End of Lawyers?* **What do you do when you're not writing about the future of the legal industry?**

I spend most of my time advising large law firms and in-house corporate legal departments. I also speak in public about the future of legal services in many countries around the world. That's how I make my living. On top of this, I advise various governments and judiciaries. And I should add that I have a new book coming out in 2013—*Tomorrow's Lawyers*—which is directed largely at young and aspiring lawyers.

What are you excited about now?

For thirty years, I've been involved in thinking about how technology would change legal practice and the administration of justice. It's been a long struggle, thinking through the ways in which the profession might modernize. In 1996, I wrote *The Future of Law*, a twenty-year prediction, and so I've got a few years to go to see if my predictions come to pass. I'll be couple of years off, I suspect, but a lot of what I wrote which was then viewed as insane will be proven, I expect, to have been not far off the mark, particularly in regards to the role of technology in bringing about change. In the '80s, I was interested in technology in the law. I wrote my doctorate at Oxford then on artificial intelligence and the law. In the '90s, I joined a law firm and became interested in strategy and change, with technology as the main (but not the only) driver. I've watched lawyers' attitudes change and adapt over the years. Technology's time has now come for the world of law. By 2016 or 2017, for example, e-discovery and online legal services will have transformed the way litigation is handled around the world. Another area of interest for me is the way in which online legal services offer answers to those who rightly agitate over the issue of access to justice. In summary, then, I'm more excited about technology now than I have been for a decade or so.

Did you think change would happen more quickly than it has in the industry?

I never expected change to be quick. That's why I was making twenty-year predictions. When you think of how change within the legal profession comes about and who brings it about, you understand that it is unlikely to come about rapidly. I'm not surprised at the modest pace. I do anticipate massive change, but it will be incremental, not like the revolution we saw in the financial sector in the '80s.

Many commentators suggest that poor global economic conditions have precipitated a lot of recent change. This is undoubtedly so, but, interestingly, when I was conducting research with GCs in 2006, I saw they were already frustrated over pricing issues. The recession has acted as a catalyst in the movement toward securing "more for less"—more legal service at less cost. I don't think this drive originated in the recession. But the recession certainly accelerated it. We were seeing signs of it much earlier. For all of us who are interested in change, it's a little bizarre that the recession has been something of a good thing: it has brought about—in hindsight, we'll see—a change in the legal profession that we needed. That is the silver lining.

What are some of the trends that are being accelerated?

By way of context, there are a few critical pressures and drivers. The first, as mentioned, is this "more for less" trend. The second is that we're moving as a society towards the internet and computer technology changing all aspects of our lives. It's naïve to think the law will be untouched by that. Third, there is the move toward the commoditization of legal services, where we shift away from one-to-one consultation to ever more polished ways of standardization and commoditization. This is a change in the mode of production. Fourth is the liberalization of the legal industry. This includes deregulation, the heavy participation of non-lawyers in legal businesses, external investment in law firms, and even high-street shops delivering legal services. The Legal Services Act 2007 will bring about this change in the UK, but awareness of its impact will also spread around the world. And its relevance will be recognized increasingly clearly as we see the ongoing effects of the recession, increasing the pressure towards getting more for less.

One phenomenon that will define the next decade in the legal world, therefore, is that clients and lawyers will have to come together and find ways to reduce costs, and this will happen at the level of the largest corporations right down to the level of individual citizens. I've been puzzling through how the profession will evolve. I think we're in a first phase of change, and this will be the longest. It will stretch from 2007 to 2014 or so. I'm talking here about medium to large firms and their clients.

What is the first phase?

Phase One is characterized by the more-for-less challenge, that is, the desire among clients to pay less for the same quality of work but in greater quantity. So far, the way this has been expressed by clients is by their going out to external firms and simply saying, "We want you to charge us less." From the point of view of in-house legal departments, in this first phase, it seems that they themselves are not going to do much changing. They'll start managing external firms more tightly and tell them they want to pay less. The main response from firms will be alternative-fee arrangements. What we're seeing in this first phase, then, is both clients and lawyers figuring out ways to stay in the old world. Clients are hoping they can continue to run their departments the way they always have, and firms might change their pricing but not the way they work.

The research I've seen suggests that the net benefits of re-tendering work and accepting alternative-fee arrangements (AFAs) results in about a 10% reduction in fees. It looks better on paper, but in reality, the reduction isn't that great. What I'm hearing from GCs is that their Boards are asking them to reduce spending by 30% to 50%. In the first phase of change that I have charted, firms and clients will gradually come to terms with the idea that AFAs grafted onto traditional in-house departments will not yield the savings needed. When most firms are proposing AFAs, they're not intending to reduce their profits. Nor are they changing the way they work. Accordingly, AFAs are the same old deal, repackaged.

Why do major law firms not change more quickly? Well, it's hard to convince a room of millionaires to change their business model. The system has worked for decades. They don't want to disrupt the old model. In this first phase, from 2007 to 2014, most firms are going to want to hang onto this old model and hope things revert to the ways of the past. But they won't. Mainstream clients will know by 2014 that they and law firms need to change radically.

Why don't GCs push harder?

Many GCs come from law firms, and they understand and are most comfortable with the old model. Some are nervous about affecting relationships with firms on whom they've relied for years. Some of them aren't clear about how to change. And that's not unreasonable in a way. Change in an industry generally comes from suppliers, not customers.

In my Phase Two, in-house counsel and firms will change pretty fundamentally. The particular change I expect will be driven by new ways of sourcing legal services: outsourcing, off-shoring, near-shoring, subcontracting to other firms, leasing lawyers, unbundling, whatever way you choose to cut it. The underpinning idea here is that you can decompose legal work into basic tasks and undertake these tasks separately but more efficiently than in the past. There are huge amounts of repetitive work in legal practice, and these routine (often administrative or process-based) tasks can be sourced at far lower cost beyond conventional law firms and in-house departments. A great deal of the work that goes on even in high-end legal work is susceptible to this kind of approach. It is a new division of labor. The key point here is that clients don't mind paying high fees for highly complex work, but they do mind paying high fees for tasks that do not require expensive lawyers in expensive firms in expensive city centers.

At the same time, clients also need to change, because all of this also applies to the work of legal departments. Clients say they want firms to change, but they also have to ask themselves if they are as efficient as they can be, and, inevitably, they must change their sourcing and methods of working as well. One key theme of Phase Two is that in-house legal departments will have to examine themselves carefully. This will not be a superficial examination. It will be a full-scale legal-needs analysis. In-house lawyers will have to identify their legal needs and dispassionately examine the best ways to resource these needs. I reckon that will take place in 2014 to 2017.

And after 2017 comes the third phase?
Yes, indeed. Phase Three is the disruptive-technology phase. This is when technology fundamentally changes the way that legal work is undertaken. Document review in litigation, for example, costs a lot. In the 1990s and 2000s, law firms derived a great deal of revenue and profit from putting junior lawyers on document-review exercises, fourteen hours a day, and charging the client much more than the firm paid these young practitioners for their work. In cases involving millions of documents and millions of emails, the cost of this approach became prohibitive. So this led to the use of paralegals instead of lawyers and the outsourcing of document review. And prices tumbled down. But now we're seeing

research that shows that intelligent discovery systems can, very approximately speaking, undertake basic review at a higher standard than human beings and at much lower cost.

Phase Two is essentially about labor arbitrage, characterized by the question, "What's the cheapest way of getting human beings to do this work?" In Phase Three, the emphasis switches to automating tasks and making work even cheaper without sacrificing quality. Thinking beyond document review, for instance, we find many transactions and agreements can be supported by automatic document assembly. In 2017, we'll be finding all sorts ways of automating low-end work and, crucially, of automating the routine elements of high-end work.

So in Phase One, we change a little but try to hang on to the old ways. Phase Two drives us fully toward new ways of sourcing legal service. And in Phase Three, we are transformed by the use of technology.

Now, I may be couple years off in my predictions for these phases, but that doesn't matter to me as a commentator. I am more concerned with defining the broad thrust of what's going to happen during this decade of transformation. I'm especially excited about new ways of sourcing legal service, about the growing impact of legal technology in client service, and about increasing access to justice for citizens. I'm also excited about the C-suite (the CEO, CFO, etc.) waking up and seeing lawyers as trusted legal advisors who can help avoid problems as well as solve them.

Do you think new legal entrepreneurs who enter the market will be more impatient and be able to change faster?

I'm approached all the time by entrepreneurs, and I understand and even welcome their impatience. I have been working closely with a private equity firm and a legal-process outsourcer, and they're impatient for change within the legal world. But there are specific cultural issues in the law and in the psyche of lawyers that don't encourage or enable rapid change. In this area more than others, it is useful to take a step back and have a conceptual structure and a deeper understanding.

Many legal software companies come into the legal market and are highly impatient and critical of lawyers' working habits. But maybe it's not the right time for their offerings. Maybe it is too early. They are often putting forward a solution that is looking for a problem. They need to match their solutions to market problems of the moment. Law firms and legal departments have to accept there's a problem before they pay for a solution.

And here's a related point about entrepreneurs: it's far harder for a mainstream law firm to change than for a start-up to launch with a new model. Entrepreneurial organizations are built on change and adaptation as the market evolves. And they even change the market themselves. They can refashion themselves to anticipate the next wave. If you're a successful law firm, however, you're an incumbent with a dilemma. If you're a global firm and you're succeeding and no one else changing, why should you risk making a change? Entrepreneurs and private-equity guys want to bake a new cake, while lawyers today still want a bigger slice of the old cake.

I always say to legal-process outsourcers that the legal market won't explode in a week. We will see huge change in the next three to five years, not the next three to five months. This is not good news for the managing partner who wants to change everything overnight or for the GC who wants firms to transform tomorrow. Well, whatever anyone's explanation for it, it's not going to happen that quickly.

Isn't it the job of upper managers in firms to see the future and prepare the firm to adapt to it?

For me, that's the difference between managers and leaders. Managers stay attuned to operational requirements: they keep the business moving and earning money. What's difficult in firms is to take a long view. Most managing partners only run the firm for a couple years, and their thinking is overwhelmingly short-term. In firms, they tend to feel that the best strategy is to do what they did last year only a little bit better; and that strategy has indeed worked for twenty-five years. So in a good market, many senior partners take the position that there's no obvious need for long-term strategy. Now that's not my view. That's the perception of law firms who have gotten along without long-term strategy. But the strategy of hoping this year will be the same as last year is no longer sufficient. If change comes from the supplier/producer and not the client, then we need different leadership within the law, people who plan for significant upheaval in the long run. It is important to remember that many law firms have been successful despite, not because of, the quality of the leadership in a good market. In a tough market, you need better leadership with clear long-term direction.

Why can't firms do what other companies do, such as set aside a small experimental unit to try out the new strategies and new technologies in mock settings and eventually in real ones?

We don't have the R&D spirit in law firms. Apple hasn't yet invented the products they're going to deliver five years from now. So too with the pharmaceuticals sector; in such a rapidly changing, intensely competitive market, they need constantly to innovate to bring something new to market every few years. Law firms, however, haven't needed to innovate to stay in the market. It's been a seller's market for decades—until recently. Now, in our buyer's market, we have to create a culture of innovation, and firms do need an R&D approach. An example of this is found in Allen & Overy, a London-based international firm. It has an innovation panel, and I sit on that panel as an external advisor. It has its own budget, and the panel's only purpose is to think about long-term innovation. Today, that is very unusual in the legal world. Very soon, it will be a necessity.

Do you look at other industries that have already changed for some sense of how the legal industry might change?

My biggest client over the last decade has been Deloitte. My first employer was Ernst & Young. People say I'm a legal futurist, when in fact what I tend to do is study other professions, like accounting, and then think about applying their success in the law. I look at technologies in other industries and how those technologies might change the legal industry. If you spend a few hours with one of the Big Four accounting firms and see what they've done in the world of tax, you get one vision of the future. In medicine, too, doctors are now unbundling tasks and multi-sourcing, offering further insight into what could be done in the law. What we have in law, though, is a dependence on insiders making changes. Any major change in the legal profession has to come from lawyers who are substantially self-regulating. That means, in effect, that they won't change that quickly.

Of course, there are lots of examples around the world of firms and in-house counsel doing some innovative stuff. I advise some firms that are really imaginative. William Gibson said, "The future has already arrived—it's just not evenly distributed yet." When people see that something new works in one arena, they wonder why it's not in operation in another place. But that takes time.

I don't think there is one future out there. I'm saying, "Here's what's likely." Now go and invent your own future.

Will the urgency to change come from younger lawyers joining the ranks?
My experience of young, up-and-coming lawyers and law students is more UK-based. When I'm invited to speak in the States, I speak at law-firm retreats or to managing partners. In the UK, I find my most conservative audiences to be law students who are cynical and skeptical about fundamental change. I don't know whether law makes you conservative or whether conservatives are drawn to law, but many law students have decided to pursue careers in the law based on often historic conceptions of lawyers and lawyering. These images are still perpetuated by media and the cinema. Students are influenced by a John Grisham/David Baldacci conception or by the many TV shows projecting highly bespoke and exciting lawyering. Although young lawyers belong to the Facebook generation, for some reason, they don't see what all this technology has to do with being lawyers.

What can law schools do to prepare students for the realities of the legal industry today?
What makes me most anxious are law professors who don't have much interest in looking at the future of legal services. There are a couple exceptions in the US and UK, but generally we don't prepare law students for the legal services that might be. So law students are unlikely to have heard, for instance, of online dispute resolution or automated document assembly or most emerging legal technologies, even though these are all coming within a

decade. We don't take time to immerse students in the possibilities, and professors regard looking a few years into the future to be beyond the legal curriculum. But we're already in a transitional period, and so it's incumbent on us to expose students to possible futures.

What are we training our young lawyers to become? In law schools, we give students the sense that all problems might reach the Supreme Court. But such cases are rare. Yes, we need to be exposed to difficult problems, but students often suffer from upper-court-itis. They don't realize that the upper-court experience is exceptional. We also need to expose students to what goes on everyday in the law office and what is likely to go on tomorrow.

There is a big review of legal education going on in England right now. I have been suggesting that approaches to training in other professions can shed useful light on legal education. Training in medicine, for example, is longer and harder now than it is in the law. You have to study for many more years and in greater depth. I find it surprising you can qualify as a solicitor in the UK after two years studying and two years as a trainee in an office. This would be unimaginable in other professions such as architecture or medicine. That does trouble me. There are some interesting questions that need to be more fully discussed about the revival of the apprenticeship system and whether there might be a better way of learning the legal trade. Law firms say even the brightest graduates with the best results are invariably ill-equipped on arrival to handle clients. I wonder whether, after the completion of professional exams, aspiring lawyers should be required to spend a year working in a firm, literally at the same desk as a partner, learning the nature of everyday work and how to interact with clients. I speak more for legal education in the UK.

To repeat my central point about legal education, I worry, in short, that we are letting our students down. Twenty-five years hence, we know legal services will be radically different. Surely our law schools should be engaging our young lawyers in thinking more systematically about their future.

Fred H. Bartlit

FOUNDING PARTNER
BARTLIT BECK HERMAN
PALENCHAR & SCOTT LLP
DENVER, CO

"Relying on highly experienced, highly trained, and highly motivated people means we want to be paid for results, not for how long it takes us."

What's your business model?

We started our model twenty years ago. We expected that competitors would match us within five years. Surprisingly, no other firm has even attempted to match us. And it is interesting that most of our competitors do not understand our model.

When I was at Kirkland Ellis and was one of the top people in litigation, it dawned on me that almost all the work preparing for trial was being done by associates who had never before seen a trial in their lives. (I'm talking about litigation, by the way; I think the problems in the law are in litigation, not transactions.) A lot of the work was being done by lawyers with no experience in doing the work.

In big law firms, their models have been to keep associates inexperienced. Big firms would hire 200 associates, and eight or nine years later, there would be four or five left. There was no incentive to mentor, because almost no one was permanent. Experience was not valued. In this bizarre eight-years-and-out associate model, the workforce that prepares for trial is perpetually kept inexperienced. I thought back then, "If there's anything in the world where experience counts, it's in trial work."

I got to thinking: what about a model based on using experienced people instead of rookies? Why not four experienced partners rather than ten inexperienced associates on the case? It goes without saying. We want to improve quality, and, by definition, if inexperienced people do the work, then quality is going to be less than it could be.

So what if we got rid of the up-and-out model and kept experienced people? Ideally, we would have all partners, no associates—the opposite of the big-firm model.

These big firms are great firms. Those running the firms are my friends.

But what if, instead of 200 hires, we hire two of the very best, and they are overwhelmingly permanent? I then have a huge incentive to train and mentor people, to impart life lessons and all that, and to insure that they are in court trying cases and know what they're doing. Quality goes up, and it costs less, because experienced people are more efficient.

Efficiency actually improves quality.

I sit for three days in typical conferences on issues in law firms. I never hear the word *quality* mentioned.

What we do is a classic Peter Drucker innovation. Let's say in an old-style large firm, an associate is told to prepare a cross-examination. The associate wants to impress a partner with his thoroughness, so he writes a 90-page cross, but there's no focus on what needs to come out at trial. So he spends ten days on the cross-exam, gives it to the chief trial lawyer, a partner who spends more time. The only guy who knows what is needed in court is the trial lawyer, who has to start over before the trial, so how inefficient is that?

How big is the firm?

We're about fifty-four partners and twelve associates. Now that we have the higher quality and much greater efficiency driven by experience, the last thing we want to do is charge by the hour.

Relying on highly experienced, highly trained, and highly motivated people means we want to be paid for results, not for how long it takes us. We make big use of technology, because we don't have associates to lean on, so the partners have to be skilled in modern technology. Twenty years ago, when I prepared a cross, it took me ten times as long to prepare it than today. We have learned to do it better and faster. We have lots of cases where there are no associates, just partners. Three experienced lawyers can do what fifteen inexperienced, rookie associates can.

How do you put teams together?

We look for people who have not worked together yet, and we get cross-fertilization in the firm. We mix people with different experiences with different partners, so everyone shares information and experience and is constantly learning and growing.

How do you price your services?

Our fee deals mean we share in a good result, and we share in a downside result. So in every single case, every fee deal is separately negotiated to address the unique facets of that litigation, but they're all based largely on sharing in good and bad results.

Do different partners negotiate the fee arrangements?

Skip Herman runs our fee negotiations. We have no committees. It's one guy doing it all. We know how many lawyers can handle a particular case. I go to meetings with very smart GCs, and I ask, "What do you think the deposition of an expert witness costs?" I get guesses ranging from $10,000 to a hundred grand. They have no database or metrics on what things should cost. They have no idea if results vary with different models of ways to achieve the result.

The GCs work for corporations who know within five decimal points what a gallon of gas or a pound of ball bearings costs to make. Here in the litigation business, which is probably a $200 billion business, nobody has any idea what something should cost. There are no metrics, just gut reactions.

Do you ever bill by the hour?

A couple years ago, a prominent trial lawyer told the *Wall Street Journal* that no good trial attorney would work except by the hour. I asked the *American Lawyer* to set up a debate with this guy, and we can state our sides. And the guy said yes, but then he backed out and said he didn't have time.

This is the science of paradigm shifts. The person who's been the most successful in the old paradigm is the last to shift to the new paradigm.

So do young people get it faster?

I see young women who are heads of litigation and who are GCs, and they seem to understand what we're doing more readily than the traditional sixty-year-old guy who spent years at a big law firm.

Everyone is a captive of their experience. Younger people and younger women see this more quickly. Lawyers are trained to see what's wrong with something. They are good at sitting in meetings and thinking of all the reasons it's not going to work. Thomas Sager at DuPont gets it. They can hire anyone they want to, and they like our model. Paul Beach at United Technologies in Hartford, he gets it.

Do you still have to work to persuade clients of the benefits of your model?

There are Fortune 10 companies who want to hire us, and they've said they only want to pay us by the hour, and we say, "No," and they can't believe it. I said to one company, "What if I can get rid of this antitrust case in six months instead of five years?" And they said they could not set up a deal where, if I were to get rid of the case in six months, we could get a flat amount for this success. They didn't hire me. I had an idea, and I told my idea to one of their young inside lawyers, and they got rid of the case in three months.

So it's not only law firms who are not letting go of the billable hour. Corporate clients are hanging on as well.

It's very hard for someone successful in a business model to scrap that model and start over. I'm a big Peter Drucker fan, and he asks, "What are good innovations?" The best innovation is one that exploits a market anomaly. In the law, the metric of time as a measure of quality is an anomaly. Measuring hours instead of results is an anomaly. To increase efficiency means you have to do it better and faster. Our model simply exploits these bizarre anomalies. We are paid according to efficiency and quality instead of time.

There's no other business where quality isn't measured by results but about how many inexperienced people you can put on a job and how long they can take to do it. A lot of the world is convinced that time is the metric for quality. People ask me why GCs at large corporations don't get my model. It's because they came from big firms, and hourly billing is what they're used to. They think thirty associates are better than ten. I've had guys who worked for me at Kirkland, and they went off to become GCs, and they still regard putting more lawyers on a case as better.

Why haven't other firms simply copied your model?

Michael Porter, a professor at Harvard, said exploiting a market anomaly is great, but the absolute best strategy is one that can't be readily matched by your top competitors. That's our model.

Why can't great law firms match our model? Because associates alone have no value, but training associates to become experienced trial lawyers has huge value. If you have a big building and lots of associates, you have to come up with a small group of experienced people in order to match our model. They do not exist now, because this is not their model.

If you're the head of the firm and you're making $4 to $6 million a year and you've got seven to eight years to make this big money, are you going to change to a new model with far fewer associates and with more work going to partners?

There are all kinds of reasons they can't do this, from what to do with all the excess real estate to how to convince partners they will be better off doing more of the important work themselves. Everywhere I go, I stand up and I ask, "Is there any firm that represents Fortune 50 clients in billion-dollar cases that cannot be hired to work by the hour?" No hands go up. We don't work by the hour, because we think it's a bad model. We're the only ones who follow this approach 100%. We're not doing this for sport. We're doing this because quality is higher, our lifestyle is way better, our young people lead better lives, and they get to do great work. Nobody's matched this, because they cannot match it without doing major surgery on their firms and their culture.

Will this change?

There's not going to be any change in my lifetime, I don't think. When I was a US Army Ranger at Fort Benning, I learned that a small band of highly experienced, highly motivated people will achieve more than armies of rookies. There's room for other models, like Jones Day. When you walk into Jones Day, it's reliable, and there's a certain degree of predictable competence no matter where you are in the world. That adds some efficiencies in quickly finding counsel all around the world. Lawyers get where they are by being successful at the ways it's always been done, not by innovating.

It is sort of like in the military. When I was an officer, I would say to my NCOs, "Let's try *that*," and they'd say, "But, Lieutenant, we've always done it *this* way."

Why don't more people take advantage of the market opportunity?

The market for movies every year for tickets is about $9 or $10 billion. In law cases and corporate litigation, it's $200 billion or more. It's a gigantic market with no metrics and little understanding of how to do things better.

The need for a new model is greater in litigation than in transaction work. The reason is because experience counts. There are a lot of transactional lawyers who close deals all the time. In transactions, they close thousands of deals, and they want to get transactions closed in a timely way, with only so much due diligence, whereas in litigation, the amount of due diligence they can spend time on would blow your mind.

But there are not that many experienced people in litigation. In the past, something like 15,000 cases were tried in the federal system, and now it is roughly 5,000. Fewer cases being tried means fewer experienced litigators, and less experience means less efficiency and lower quality.

How do you recruit lawyers?

We do no recruiting. It's all word of mouth. Every person we hire contacts us. We don't do any entertaining, no visits to law schools, no summer program. Word gets around about our different way of doing things. Our culture and model means that personal life is way better.

What moves, if any, did you make during the recession?

We didn't do anything—nothing at all. We saw amazing things going on out there. We don't have that many big repeat clients. We have one-off projects. We're always competing with the same suspects around the country on these big matters. And there were big deals where big firms were saying they wouldn't charge anything for the first year. They'd do the work for practically nothing to keep their associates busy. Not much surprises me, but during the lowdown level of the recession, there were deals like this being made all the time.

Do you hear about new trends in the legal industry from GCs?

No, but I have another idea. We don't want to be big. I have dinner with all of our people regularly, and our model is to stay small. We get offers to merge. But we don't want to do that.

We want to get the work done. A lot of terrific young women are out there, and they've gone to top schools, worked at top firms, but left to go home and raise kids. There's a huge labor resource of talented women at home who could be great lawyers if we can figure out how to use them. I made a deal with a young woman in our firm so she can work part-time from home. I send an email to her from a meeting I'm in, and she finds the answer. When we're shorthanded at trials, we bring her in, and she participates. She comes into the office so she can stay part of our culture. She may never come back full-time, but that's fine. People are offshoring to India, but America is full of women who would sit down at home three hours a day to do document review and love it.

How have you dealt with document review?

People are setting up big document factories, and what big firms love is a monster document case with 300 depositions. We don't like this kind of case. We like a case that's going to be tried.

We want to use our skills and make a difference. We've figured out a way to work with other firms, but this is not our best model, the big document case. We've set up computers, and we have software we use to do document review efficiently. We have to keep competing, and we do think about ways to innovate.

Do you have any turnover at the firm?
No one has ever left our firm to go to a competing large law firm. We have had some people leave for startups. There is no competing for partnerships in our model, because everyone's a partner. When you have internal competition for partnership, you have low morale. We have great morale.

I'm always surprised lawyers aren't more eager to let go of the billable hour, because chasing hours takes over your personal life as well as your working life.
I used to think that trial work ought to be the most enjoyable way to make a living. The issues are fascinating, the stakes are high, you work in small teams, and great ideas can come from anywhere, anytime. So I thought it should be a great way to make a living, but it can be the worst, because most young lawyers sit in the office, draft memos that are never used, and review documents. You're canned inside a room, with no real input and no training, no mentoring. You never go to trial, your main skill is writing mean letters, and you become a mean, unhappy person.

In a firm like ours, where you work cases all the time, you will experience something totally different from that. You will see your work played out in court. You will learn. We don't charge by the hour, and so if you go into our offices in the evening, you won't see anyone. They go home. They see their families. They work in the evening at home from the computer. There's no reason for face time. There's not a soul in our offices on the weekend. Why would there be?

In the old days at Kirkland, we'd all come to the office on Saturday to write a brief. We'd dictate a brief to the secretary, eat pizza while she typed, do another draft, and be there all day considering ourselves warriors. Now I'm up at four, I send out a draft, and I go work out at the gym. Sean Gallagher receives the draft at home, he goes to his kids' soccer game, edits the draft, and sends it to me. It enables us to work when we want to work without having to be in some particular place wasting time.

What kind of pressure are GCs under today?
Occasionally, I see companies with financial pressures put pressures on the law department, and these pressures are so great that they push the legal department to become more interested in price than quality. People have a good lawsuit at some companies, and they don't pursue it, because they don't want a monthly hit to their earnings. The eventual big win is not as important as the monthly hit which impacts earnings in real time.

How do you convince GCs to hire you to pursue a case?
Here's an example of what our deals are like. We sit with a sophisticated company, and we say we'll do this case for $200,000 per month instead of the $300,000 per month a big firm would charge. And we'll use experienced attorneys, not new associates, and you can put your extra $100,000 in an account.

If we perform efficiently, we can earn our discount (or a multiple of the discount) back for good results. The financial people love it, because they like predictable costs and no surprises. If the case comes to a halt, we don't charge for a month if we don't do any work. If the case goes to appeal, and there's no work being done, we don't send a bill when we're not working. What the client pays is reasonably commensurate with the results they get. In some cases, we leave it to the client to pay us a multiple of the discount based on professional trust for what we've achieved in terms of quality and efficiency.

This is, to me, such common sense that it's hard to imagine people not getting it. But I've talked endlessly to people at meetings and conferences, and they still don't get it. GCs have even told me that, years ago, it was typical for a law firm to bill a client for years, make all the money to be made, and figure there was no additional value to try the case. So they'd send a letter to the GC just before trial to end it. That's it.

Unlike that kind of firm, we have absolutely no incentive to do unnecessary work. We have incentive to prevail. If we have the incentive to do unnecessary work and earn the same amount whether we win or lose, that's bad. If there is no financial motivation for success, there will be less success, of course.

So if you want to win, and your lawyers like going to trial, then you must not take on every case.

We often put $100,000 in due diligence on whether or not to try a case. We don't want to take on losers and kill ourselves for three years for a losing case. Maybe we can keep the verdict down, and that's the point, but we want to know what kind of case we're working on. We want cases suited to us. We want cases for trial. But at typical big firms, they never turn cases down, because they get paid no matter what. We review our cases in depth, and we may decide never to bring a case.

We believe you get better results with a small team of expert lawyers who are highly experienced and enjoy taking cases to trial.

Rodolfo Parga, Jr.

CEO, MANAGING SHAREHOLDER
RYLEY CARLOCK & APPLEWHITE
PHOENIX, AZ

"Lawyers are always assessing risk and finding ways to limit it, but sometimes being a good entrepreneur is not about that. It's about taking a leap of faith and forging ahead on some of these fronts. All of us have to deal with a new reality. That reality includes alternative fees, new operating models, unbundling, and defining and building new client relationships."

How were you and your firm affected by the recession?
I've been in Phoenix for twenty years with the same firm. I grew up in Sante Fe, New Mexico, and went to Amherst College in Massachusetts and law school at the University of New Mexico. It has taken Phoenix longer to come out of the Great Recession than a lot of other states, especially the housing market. Nevada is in a similar situation with the housing market. We have been working through a lot of foreclosure inventory over the past couple of years, but things are beginning to improve. We see a lot of Canadian

buyers and investors coming in, because of the good exchange rate and the favorable housing deals that exist.

The firm has 115 attorneys and does work inside and outside the state. We are regional with some national practices. We've been established since 1948. There's a long history here. The lion's share of our work is from this region. We have offices in Phoenix, Denver, and Grand Rapids. The Grand Rapids office is our Eastern office for our document-control group. We also have a Western office located in Phoenix for our document-control group. We do document-control work, including both electronic and paper review, for large multi-national companies out of Phoenix and Grand Rapids.

What do you see five years from now in the industry?

I think that the next big trend is a continuation of what's already been identified. There's going to be more unbundling of different types of legal services. Any work that's more repetitive in nature will come under more and more pressure to be unbundled from the traditional core practice of law. I also think we'll see more of the staff-attorney model. That will gravitate more to virtual offices of attorneys. Law firms will find ways to bring in talented individuals who may not be housed in brick and mortar buildings. Teams of attorneys may be employed by or affiliated with a law firm, but those attorneys will work in virtual offices from their homes or elsewhere. The staffing of particular cases or matters will be quite different.

Will this redefine what it means to be a solo attorney?

You'll have teams of attorneys with particular expertise, like intellectual property, and the attorney will be somewhere else in a virtual office. That attorney can then be contracted with, consulted on cases and issues, and that's how the relationship will work. Taking it one step further, you can see an analogy to a freelance writer: that same IP attorney will have the ability to work for multiple law firms, subject to conflicts of interest and confidentiality, but those individuals with expertise may be independent contractors who come in and out of the law firm of the future.

That brings up a kind of entrepreneurship that lawyers may have to learn.

Lawyers are always assessing risk and finding ways to limit it, but sometimes being a good entrepreneur is not about that. It's about taking a leap of faith and forging ahead on some of these fronts. Six, seven years ago, firms had the luxury of maintaining their current paths, but, for the most part, I don't think that luxury exists anymore. All of us have to deal with a new reality. That reality includes alternative fees, new operating models, unbundling, and defining and building new client relationships.

Are law schools preparing graduates for this new reality?

It's challenging for students coming out of law school right now. My daughter is a teenager, but if she were a college senior thinking about law school, I'd probably have a very in-depth conversation with her about whether or not the timing is right. Maybe three years from now, it'll be a little different. There's a lot of overcapacity right now, with the models changing, and the amount of debt is a burden. So from a return perspective for any individual student, it's very challenging.

I think law still presents good opportunities for individuals who understand and are prepared to deal with the new reality in the legal market. I would counsel anyone thinking of law school to take undergraduate business courses, get some working experience in business, or, more ideally, consider a double JD/MBA route, though that's not for everyone. People most able to distinguish themselves will be those who have sound business backgrounds and have an entrepreneurial spirit.

Your firm is unique. It has a practice group that provides document review and unbundling services. How did this start?

We established our document-control group in the Phoenix facility in 2005. One of our clients, a Fortune 200 company, was faced with the departure of its in-house head of litigation, and they wanted someone from our firm to help out until they found a replacement. We saw it as an opportunity to better understand what in-house attorneys and departments were struggling with.

Bill McManus served in that role for over a year, and during that time, we were able to get a different perspective on the needs of a corporate in-house legal department. This was before the full effects of e-discovery had taken hold in the industry. Bill noticed inefficiencies in the discovery process, and he implemented positive processes in our client's legal department to manage outside law firms and try some unbundling. When Bill rejoined our firm after his tour was done at the company, we got together, with our partner Matt Clarke, and we agreed there were trends here that would transform the legal industry. Those two guys were the creative forces behind the practice group that we developed.

The group started off modestly, but over the years, it has become a more important component of the firm, in terms of providing services to clients and in overall productivity of the group in relation to the firm. We serve some AMLaw 100 law firms with their unbundling needs, and we also work directly with all sizes of companies for document-control needs.

What kind of model supports these two functions within one firm?

Our model is different. We haven't split the entity in any corporate way. The practice group is just like any other functioning part in the firm. We wanted a model to encourage and facilitate seamless services at a law firm. So to do that, we kept that practice group under the same umbrella as the law firm, which afforded us the best opportunities to serve clients.

Why did you open your document-review office in Grand Rapids?

We definitely had a lot of encouragement and support from the local government to go into Grand Rapids. From a talent-pool perspective, we saw an opportunity in Michigan. The state has great law schools but was in economic pain. We could get top quality individuals at a good value, and we could pass that value on to clients.

What does your document-control group do exactly?

Our document-control group is unique in that it offers three types of services:
    (1) e-review, which deals with electronic discovery;
    (2) paper review, in which case we occasionally have

literally thousands of banker's boxes of paper files to evaluate; and

(3) document retention, where we advise clients about what documents to maintain according to what regulations.

We provide services on all three fronts. Our competitors offer one or two of these, but not many offer all three. Clients come to us because we are a one-stop shop.

Offering all three, we tend to get bigger company clients with more frequent litigation. For a lot of companies, half the battle is being advised on what they have. We've had situations where boxes are being pulled out of warehouses that haven't been touched in decades. People have to wear protective gloves and other safety devices, because some of the information is so old. We try to get a good handle on what the company has and when they can start getting rid of it. In some cases, a company will keep material in certain facilities, and we'll find things from several decades ago. They'll discover a history people had forgotten long ago. It's kind of cool from a historical perspective.

Can you give an example of how this works?

If we are engaged on a matter, the matter will come through our two co-founding attorneys, Bill McManus or Matt Clarke. One of them will be the point individual on the engagement. There will be a meeting to evaluate the scope of project. We'll develop models to identify the scope and what needs to be done so we can give the client an idea of the staffing needs and cost. The project will be overseen by project managers, who are licensed attorneys. Our project managers have been with us for several years, some since the beginning of the group. The project managers are the point people on a daily basis for the operation, whether the project is in Phoenix or Grand Rapids.

We have different models of quality testing. We're constantly taking samples of search results to make sure we have strict quality control over the type of review being done and the results. The lengths of projects vary greatly. Some projects are urgent. Let's say a petition for injunctive relief has been filed in a case, and the court orders an expedited discovery. That means we work 24/7 to get that information. Other engagements are multi-year, with such a massive quantity of information being reviewed that it takes many months to go through.

How do you play the advisor role?

It's always been part of our plan to keep a close eye on things. We want to implement well and work well as time goes on. We are very proactive in terms of counseling a national client regarding many issues involving discovery, and we do it in a timely and uniform manner. For example, we may work on a case filed in Ohio and one in Washington state, and we make sure the client is given uniform approaches on both cases to avoid inconsistencies on the type of response. It's critical to make sure everyone is on the same page.

Do you send any work overseas?

We have to confront, on a daily basis, the reality that some of this work is being sent overseas, to India and otherwise. We've based our platform on extracting value from the significant advantages of having work performed stateside by licensed attorneys trained in American law schools. Some of our staff attorneys come from the largest firms in the country. Some are former judges, former government attorneys, and private attorneys. At last count, we have people who speak ten languages. We've done translations in Japanese, Mandarin Chinese, Korean, and Spanish. We have an exceptionally talented core group. By sending something overseas, you might save a buck here or there, but you risk losing control over quality and responsiveness. If you keep work here, you can get a plane anytime you want and check the work being done, and the client can do that as well.

What does the staff say they like about the work?

They enjoy the challenging environment of doing detective work. Some people have told me they enjoy finding a needle in the haystack. Many enjoy having flexibility in their lifestyle. They don't have to wear a suit. They can find scheduling that works for them. Some work a night shift; it's their choice. Unbundling and technology are driving this different model, and it's never going back to the way it was before. All paper is going electronic. All of it will be put in an e-format.

The legal industry has been transformed where certain types of legal work are going to be performed under different models. For new law graduates, the idea of working within models based on unbundling will be more of the norm. I think a firm has to embrace the different models out there and provide legal services to clients in a variety of ways. What this transformation has taught us is that clients are demanding more and more value.

How do you define value?
Value can be translated into different models: the billable hour, alternative fees based on flat fees or hybrid agreements, an unbundled model based on staff attorneys. A firm has to find models at any given time that provide the most value to that particular client. Resistant law firms are going to find it more and more difficult to be successful in the near future. Law firms that embrace creativity in optimizing value for the client will continue to be successful.

At our firm, we were ahead of the curve in document control. So by the time the recession came around, we were already doing the things other firms were only starting to talk about doing. This has not been a fundamental change for us. It's more of an evolution of what we were already doing.

The staff-attorney model may be more the norm for law grads, but there will be other models in firms in which lawyers can fit differently. Regardless of the model, everything will be driven by value. There's no getting away from that. Even if firms try to keep doing work on a billable-hour basis, clients will be applying a much higher level of scrutiny than law firms have previously dealt with. Firms are under serious pressure to prove to their clients that they're getting good value.

How is your relationship with GCs right now?
This has strengthened our relationships with existing clients. They say, "Hey, you listen to us. You're responsive to our needs. We needed to do this, and you partnered with us to get it done." It's also opened doors to opportunities with other prospective clients. I think there's a real desire on the part of the corporate clients. They want firms to demonstrate that they can be sound business partners, just as they are.

I think the view of insisting on more models will be the more prevalent view. GCs want more efficiency without sacrificing quality. In our experience, we're getting GCs coming to us not necessarily dictating that we need to do ABC to keep the work. It's much more along the lines of: "This is where we need to be." They need to report their control of the legal budget back to their superiors. And the GC can come to the firm and help figure out how to get to that budget. That's where we can provide value by being creative and open to a variety of models. It's much more a partnership with an open discussion.

Veta T. Richardson

PRESIDENT AND CHIEF EXECUTIVE OFFICER
ASSOCIATION OF CORPORATE COUNSEL (ACC)
WASHINGTON, DC

"General counsel now act as full and equal members in their C-suites. They're defining the value of their legal departments. They're now expected to contribute to the bottom line and add value."

You have been President and CEO of the Association of Corporate Counsel (ACC) since July 2011. What is your role?

Along with the ACC Board of Directors, I am responsible for charting and implementing ACC's strategic plan and vision for the future. When I arrived in 2011, we launched a year-long strategic planning process. We spent time collecting data, soliciting the views of our members, holding focus groups, and understanding our members. Our goal at the ACC is to understand the needs of our membership and build a stronger value proposition to serve our members better. We adopted ACC's new five-year strategic plan in February of 2012, and since then we have been focused on its execution.

What were you doing before you joined the ACC as president?

When I came to this job, I was going full circle. I started my career out of law school as an ACC member working at Sunoco for Don Walsh, one of the ACC's founders. He, along with a group of top GCs, founded the ACC in 1982. I worked as in-house counsel at Sunoco from 1986–1997 where my focus was securities law, finance, corporate governance and transactions. I left Sunoco to move to DC and work for ACC as one of the vice presidents reporting to Fred Krebs, then-president of ACC. In 2001, I left ACC to serve as the head of the Minority Corporate Counsel Association (MCCA) for a decade. When Fred Krebs announced he was retiring as ACC president, I applied for the position, and now I'm back at the ACC. It's really gratifying to be part of an association that has played such an instrumental role in my career.

How did you move from Sunoco to the ACC in the Nineties?

I had an interest in relocating from Philadelphia where Sunoco was headquartered to Washington, DC, because I had fallen in love with DC while I was in college and law school in the area. At Sunoco, I was doing securities, finance, mergers and acquisitions, and disclosure work. As a member, I went to the ACC's annual meeting in DC in 1996 with the intent of connecting with more people. I met Fred Krebs, who was then the president of the ACC. He wanted to create a department focusing on member services to add value. He was looking for a senior-level attorney from a large law department to create those services, including a virtual law library. I interviewed for the position and started at the ACC in March 1997.

How was your experience at that time at the ACC?

I guess my expectations were met and more. I found that I really enjoyed the service aspect of bar-association life: thinking about problems that in-house counsel have in their practice of law and how the ACC could help solve those problems. I enjoyed thinking about issues not in terms of one client and one set of issues, but instead looking expansively at broad categories of law-practice problems and types of challenges. I found that stimulating intellectually, as it was a very creative role.

You ended up doing what you wanted to do?
   Yes, but not because I knew it was what I wanted to do. I always thought that I wanted to become a corporate lawyer for a Fortune 500 company and have a very transactions-oriented, in-house practice. And I was fortunate to do that. But after Sunoco, my view of myself as a professional evolved, and I started to view myself and my opportunities in a broader way than the way I was used to doing. There was a fear factor when I was going into the uncharted territory of nonprofit association management. But it was a calculated risk. I was using my in-house skills to serve the community, and for me, it's a risk that worked out quite well.

Why did you move from the ACC to the MCCA?
   It was a tremendous opportunity. I had grown to know and enjoy association life and nonprofit-management issues. The MCCA had presented an opportunity to run and change an organization, as well as influence the legal profession to become more diverse. It was taking a big leap. But it offered me a chance to really develop my leadership and management skills, working with an outstanding board of directors. I was stepping farther away from the traditional practice of law again, and the ACC was the initial bridge that helped me feel comfortable doing that. I saw myself and my opportunities a lot differently. I found I enjoyed the fast-pace, high-level of responsibility and strategic aspects of being a CEO. I was thinking as a business executive, and lawyers were advising me. I really enjoyed it. I believe each one of us could do several different jobs in a career span and do them well and find them fulfilling. Life is a function of where you choose to focus your attention and time at any one point, and for me now, it's association management.

Because you have a perspective spanning your years with the ACC and MCCA, what issues in the business of law have remained persistent ones?
   Managing outside counsel remains a persistent issue and responsibility. In-house counsel have always grappled with how to most effectively manage their outside counsel. One reason corporations establish an in-house law department is to oversee the relationship with outside counsel and manage the costs paid

to the law firms they retain. In-house counsel are always looking to derive greater value from their outside-counsel relationships. That's as true today as it was in 1986 when I went in-house.

How have outside counsel pricing discussions evolved?

It used to be that law firms would send invoices with very little information. They would rarely break down their services. Over time, that's evolved, and the GC has become much more involved with the oversight of outside-counsel spend.

Today, we see in-house counsel discussing whether or not the billable hour is a sustainable model and redefining their approaches to outside-counsel retention away from hourly billing. The ACC has been front and center in advancing that dialogue since 2007 or 2008, the timing of which coincided with the financial crisis, and those hard economic times helped fuel the discussion around how to lower costs without diminishing quality of service.

It's now common for in-house counsel to discuss models beyond the billable-hour model, and we've seen a greater level of receptivity among firms. A greater number of corporations each year are examining instances where alternatives make sense. And it's about real alternatives, not just looking for discounts on hourly fees.

How is the role of general counsel evolving today?

General counsel are now assuming roles in which they act as full and equal members in their C-suites. They're looking to demonstrate and enhance their skill set beyond simply being effective lawyers. They're defining the value of their legal departments beyond being an expense or cost center within the company. The general counsel is more than a gatekeeper keeping outside legal costs down. They're now expected to contribute to the bottom line and add value.

How do you define value for in-house counsel?

I think that value is defined from the perspective of those whom we serve: business executives, boards of directors, organizations, shareholders or members. We have to remain relevant, meet their needs, anticipate their needs, see what trends are on the horizon, and make sure the client remains in the best position. In-house counsel need to be engaged early on with the clients in order for the client to fully utilize the skills and abilities of the in-house counsel. I would define *providing value* as consistently meeting or exceeding needs and expectations, and to do that, the in-house counsel needs to be involved in a comprehensive way in order to perform as an advocate and advisor and provide value.

What can law schools do to prepare students to enter the legal industry today?
Students need greater exposure to the practical realities, not just the legal theories, associated with practicing law. In fact, Fred Krebs, my predecessor, is now a senior fellow at the Georgetown Center for the Study of the Legal Profession. We have a group of members, including Fred, who teach practice-oriented courses, and they come together at the ACC's annual meeting. They share syllabi and bring their practical perspectives to curricula design. Students are exposed to what client service means in practice. They learn it doesn't mean providing an exhaustive memo. There are lots of gray areas in many circumstances that require good judgment in order to get to an answer or make a recommendation. So to be an effective advocate or counsel for your client, you really need to understand the client's business and goals in order to help the client achieve those goals within the parameters of the law.

What advice would you give to graduating law students?
They have to think of themselves more flexibly than law graduates did a generation ago. They have to think about their skill sets more expansively. They have to think about volunteer opportunities and keep up networks. The people in the best positions to find jobs they enjoy are people who take the time to be involved, who join communities and volunteer, and who go beyond the academic setting or any traditional model in their industry.

They should take time to be involved in a clinical experience, maybe working *pro bono* through their school or an academic clinic. Students who make investments in themselves come out with practical knowledge and practical ways of working with others. It's not good enough these days to go through the traditional, academic law-school curriculum and say you have great grades and you were on law review. Those skills don't translate into anything that's marketable today over the long term of a career.

I think someone who has more practical knowledge and experience, who has actual work experience, who has represented clients and met their client's expectations—they have the skills to hit the ground running.

Do you think employers and firms are evaluating the wrong kinds of information when hiring?

Information is valuable, but too much information is not so valuable. When information causes us to benchmark against one another and be too critical of our own experience, we've gone too far. For example, ranking law schools and categorizing people's potential according to where they graduate, these go too far. In 1986 when I graduated, they weren't ranking law schools. There was no *US News & World Report* ranking yet. So everyone looked at people more in terms of their unique situations and experiences.

Fast forward. My sister graduated in 1996, and there were new websites called Greedy Associates and others that allowed associates to benchmark their salaries and rank their law firms. This kind of ranking and comparison creates dissatisfaction, although most students fresh out of law school and working at a law firm make great income for their age and experience. But when associates started comparing firm salaries, it triggered a ridiculous competition.

It's the same thing with profits per partner. When profits per partner began to be published, the information created a free-agency system that was not about partnership but about position. Firms made decisions based upon how best to sustain and prop up those profits per partner. I don't think it's a healthy way to decide who should be a part of the partnership. I think it's damaging.

Do you think law graduates today should get some business experience?

I definitely think the experience would help. The challenge in this economy, if you're able to come out of school and get a position in an organization, is to understand at the entry level how organizations are run. It's beneficial to learn customer-service skills in dealing with the public. They're important and should perhaps be learned prior to law school. If I were graduating from college now, I don't know if I'd go to law school right away, but college graduates are entering the marketplace in a difficult time. Maybe they're going to law school right away because they can't find a job.

What about entrepreneurial experience?

We don't deal with entrepreneurs in terms of startup companies, but we do try to encourage lawyers to acquire skills in entrepreneurship. There are sales and marketing roles within legal-services providers, and those companies are looking for people to fill those jobs.

I see a trend in which more lawyers are taking positions as compliance officers in organizations. They report back to law departments, but they're using their knowledge of regulatory process to find ways to reduce risk and liability for organizations.

Another area where I see lawyers moving is lawyers who have an interest in human resources. Lawyers are working up to become vice presidents in human resources. HR has many positions. There are chief diversity officers and chief talent officers, and a good number of lawyers are being selected to fill these roles in corporations. And some positions are global, too. Some organizations are more often considering people from outside the U.S. for human-resources and management positions.

What big trends do you see coming up in next two to three years?

The value-challenge discussion will evolve. We will see more companies and law firms move away from hourly models. As the practice of law becomes increasingly global, new models and new entrants in client-service models will assist in stimulating change. Technology connects us all over the world. At one time, it was unheard of to outsource document review all over world, and now it's commonplace. New models in other areas will cause people to step back and rethink the *status quo*.

Richard Fields

CHAIRMAN OF THE BOARD OF DIRECTORS
JURIDICA CAPITAL MANAGEMENT, INC.
NEW YORK, NY

"I think our business is about to have a really interesting period. I'm excited about where we are. I think very soon we will have proven the concept not just to lawyers and general counsel but also to investors."

What does Juridica do?
It's simple, but complex. The simple idea is that a lawsuit is a commercial claim that can be bought and sold. A commercial investor can buy an interest in a lawsuit. The investment shifts some of the risk, provides cash flow for the case, and gives returns to the investor as a portion of the winnings. If the case fails, the investor does not receive any money back. That's the risk. We take equity stakes in commercial claims for a share of the upside. It is another form of asset-backed financing for our corporate clients. Our clients are *Fortune* 500 companies and universities. Commercial litigation is a multi-billion dollar market with no dominant player. Litigation funding is large-scale commercial

financing. One of the commercial-litigation funders will eventually become a billion-dollar-plus player in the market.

This is a relatively new phenomenon. Are there critics?
The insurance industry is not supportive of what we are doing in litigation finance. They're concerned that investment in lawsuits will lead to more frivolous lawsuits. Given the insurance industry's concerns, we avoid investing in cases with the insurance industry on the other side. In fact, we have two cases in which insurance companies are plaintiffs. We tend to invest in cases involving patents, antitrust issues, trade secrets, and general commercial disputes. We do not invest in class actions, mass-tort, or personal-injury cases.

What other companies in the U.S. are doing what you're doing?
Parabellum and Burford Capital are in our space. One of the first companies to do this was in Australia. There are also several patent hedge funds. Intellectual Ventures invested $2 billion into patents for litigation. Additionally, there are numerous hedge funds that invest in commercial litigation.

Do you pay attention to what's going on with the Legal Services Act in the UK?
I think the U.S. will be very slow to adopt the UK investing model in law firms. I have handled many cases in the UK, and I learned that change in the UK is evolutionary, not revolutionary. I think you'll see people investing in law firms. I think change will be slow, but I don't see any reason why—if law firms can access the debt market—they shouldn't be able to access the equity market, as long as their obligations to their clients are put ahead of their obligations to their shareholders. Australian regulators, where law firms first went public, have done a great job of sorting out these issues.

Is this sector growing fast?
It's here to stay, and it will be very large. It's a very different business from the personal-injury sector. In the commercial sector, there is wide acceptance in top-tier law firms. We have eighteen *AmLaw* 100 firms in our portfolio. We also have an increasing

acceptance among general counsel. They call us directly to partner with us, and we are seen by many as investment advisors to the general counsel's office.

We really turned the corner in 2010 and 2011. During the 2008 crash, there was increased interest, because cash was tight, and demand for our product went off the charts. On the other hand, our portfolio went long, because big cases took longer to settle. I think our business is about to have a really interesting period. I'm excited about where we are. I think very soon we will have proven the concept not just to lawyers and general counsel but also to investors.

How did Juridica start?

I was a plaintiff's lawyer for twenty-five years representing *Fortune* 500 companies suing insurance companies. It became a settlement practice. I was seeing the same people over and over again in cases and depositions. At my law firm, I developed a portfolio of investments in contingency-fee cases, and the cases had a variety of alternative-fee structures. I saw the benefits of diversifying risk across the portfolio and how diversifying risk affected returns, cash flow, and predictability.

By the time I was in my mid-thirties, my team and our partners in finance outside of the firm saw that litigation, like property or equipment, was simply another form of corporate asset on the balance sheet. I thought about the whole process of monetizing these things, which led to working with more economists and fewer lawyers. A team then at Arthur Andersen, lead by my friend Mark Hargis who is now CEO of Claro Consulting and still working with us, helped us build a model to value litigation risk. We had conversations with insurance companies about what they needed to settle cases. Therefore, we spent a lot of time talking with them about how to model risk and reach a settlement in a way they were comfortable with.

In 1999, I had a brilliant Ph.D. on my team at Swidler Berlin in Washington, D.C. Dr. Sunil Bala focused on information flow while others on my team focused on economics. I was trying to deliver the facts efficiently to our adversaries in order to help them evaluate risk, avoid litigation, and reach settlements. We realized that litigation was a very inefficient tool for solving business problems. And often the tool was deployed by clients without sufficient economic analysis and by lawyers without understanding the business context of the problem. Our process put economic analysis first so clients could set realistic objectives and then adapt a strategy to achieve those objectives.

One of the things that is clear about litigation is that the process of getting to the truth is expensive and inefficient. In one case, we had five million documents in a warehouse in Utah, with no air conditioning. We were suing fifty or sixty insurers. We gave the keys to the insurance companies and said, "Have fun." It took them a nice year and a half to review those documents, and we made money just dealing with this extraordinarily inefficient process, because we were paid by the hour. But from an economic perspective, it's really stupid to do it that way. Of course, this was before email, and things have changed with the focus on e-discovery and computer analysis of information, but, generally, I believe it is still true that litigation is a very inefficient way to get at the facts and evaluate risk.

In the mid-1990s, Dr. Bala designed a process for reviewing documents using software and the Internet. We told the insurance companies we wanted to settle cases more efficiently and not have them dig for facts and waste time. We organized our client's cases and gave our adversaries the key facts on a silver platter. The facts were organized, summarized, and included all our weaknesses. We convinced our clients that this was the most cost-effective way to settle their cases for the highest amount, because our focus was economics and the process was based on trust. Insurers were concerned that without litigation they would not be correctly evaluating the facts in the cases, but we told them that, if they caught us hiding the weaknesses in our cases, they were free to never settle with us again. The transparency in the process not only saved both sides millions in legal fees and years of time, but it shifted the focus to finding a fair solution based on a very open discussion about the law, the facts, and the risks.

On one occasion, a client was willing to pay us $7.5 million as an upfront retainer, plus a contingency fee, but wanted to continue behaving the same way they had been during ten years of acrimonious litigation with their insurer. We told them to keep their money, because their approach was not going to work and would harm our ability to settle for other clients. They were so shocked at our refusal to continue what they were doing that they hired us and adopted our approach. We settled for multiples of their litigation target in nine months. We did this using openness, dialogue, and decision-tree modeling. We met with clients and adversaries and handed over key documents, our risk assessments, and the results of our decision-tree models, and we told them what we thought they should pay.

After that, I discovered an arbitrage play in the insurance market. I started a company called Global Risk with my friend John Osborne in D.C. We started by trading claims against insolvent English insurers. We figured out a way to trade insurance claims, and we did very well doing it.

After I left Global Risk and returned to the U.S. in 2003, I had an idea for a fund that would invest in commercial-litigation claims and discussed it with a lawyer who advised me during that time. I wanted capital to invest in contingency cases across the whole market, not just within an individual law firm. There were compliance and ethics issues, and my co-founder of Juridica wrote a 150-page white paper addressing all these issues. I was representing General Motors at the time, and a key witness in the case was Paul Hodges, one of the most successful stockbrokers in London. We discussed our idea with Paul, and Cenkos Securities and Paul Hodges raised $160 million for us between May and December in 2007. The Juridica IPO launched on 21 December 2007.

When you invest in a case, what's the preferred outcome: a good settlement or a win at trial?

From the investors' point of view, you want predictability, so you want to invest in cases that have a high chance of settling. Because we are not running the cases and are generally passive investors, we must rely on an alignment of interests among the clients, the lawyers, and Juridica. In other words, we don't want to win when they lose, and we don't want to lose when they win. We want to be working toward the same goal. Most of our investments are structured so that investors are paid their capital out of first dollars. We also prefer investments where the lawyers are demonstrating their belief in the merits by sharing risk through an alternative-fee arrangement.

Have you noticed law firms changing the way they do business?
I think law firms have been forced to become more focused on the economic fundamentals of business. They are much, much quicker to cut staff and cut overhead, because of the turmoil in the market in 2008 and 2009. I think that's probably a good thing. What surprises me is that GCs haven't used this opportunity to change the paradigm. As an investor and lawyer, I believe the billable-hour model is seriously flawed. If I were a GC, I would rarely pay lawyers by the hour. It's not a fair way to assess value, and it creates conflicts that are not in the client's interest. The system is slow and expensive. The billable hour is bad economics and bad public policy. It has to change at some point.

Do fee structures affect what cases you invest in?
Yes. I thought the great recession was the best catalyst we could have had, and yet I still see people coming here with cases for us to invest in, and these cases still have fee structures that work to the client's disadvantage. We tell people we love the case, we love the lawyers, but it's not a proper fee arrangement. If interests are not properly aligned, we cannot invest.

Do you use some kind of analytic tool to weigh the risks and benefits of investing in any particular case?
We've been working with our economic and software team for twenty years, and together we have created several tools that we use in our investment. In the early part of our due-diligence process, we use a tool that we call our negotiation-assessment tool. We model potential returns to all parties: the fund, the lawyers, and the clients. And we test the fee arrangement to see how this plays out in multiple scenarios. We're focused on investing money in cases but also we want to bring value to the process.

That sounds like your role in these cases is more than as an investor.

We are bringing more than money to this process, but we remain a passive investor. We bring a different perspective. It's always been my dream that CFOs and GCs get together and do serious economic analysis on the front end of litigation. This is rarely done with any sort of systematic rigor in a way that would help a company determine whether or not pursuing the case was a good investment and on what terms. We like to think that we are bringing valuable analysis to help clients make better judgments.

But you stop short of giving legal advice.

We do not provide legal advice and do not interfere with the attorney/client relationship. Sometimes they invite us to share our views. If we have a view on business issues, we may share it, but we never provide legal advice.

How do you think legal education might change to accommodate changes in the industry?

The intersection between law and finance is fascinating. The problem with a legal education is that it's narrowly focused. Lawyers are at a disadvantage when they are advising on complex business in the litigation context but have no real business training or experience. They have to learn business and finance as they mature as lawyers. Bringing a financial perspective to the practice of law is of great value. Business problem solving often comes down to context. Commercial cases have commercial context, and you have to understand the human and economic sides as well as the legal issues. Why does one case settle while another does not? What factors affect human behavior in economics? You apply them to dispute resolution. The more we see a marriage between law and finance, the more efficient the process will become and the more justice will happen. For me, that's a good thing.

David B. Wilkins

Vice Dean, Global Initiatives on the Legal Profession
Director, Program on the Legal Profession
Lester Kissel Professor of Law
Harvard Law School
Cambridge, MA

"We have to be willing to rethink the role of both traditional legal education and the kind of apprenticeship and training that we have always expected the profession to provide in order to form a new and more effective partnership capable of working collaboratively together to train the next generation of lawyers."

You are the director of the Program on the Legal Profession at Harvard. What is that?

It's an academic program with three goals. First, we want to conduct cutting-edge, world-class empirical research on changes in the industry. Second, we want to change the way that law schools teach, from developing innovative courses to sustaining a lecture series with visiting speakers from around the world. Our center and New York Law School worked in a joint venture to host a series of three conferences on the future of legal education.

And third, we want to build bridges between the academy and the profession.

What are the major changes in the legal industry?

There are a few organizing principles. Globalization has transformed the law from a network of local, small, fragmented providers to large-scale global providers with cross-border transactions on the national and global scales. This has resulted in changes in the sizes of organizations. In 1968, Shearman and Sterling was the largest firm in the world with 165 attorneys, and now we have firms with 3,000 and 4,000 attorneys. Law is increasingly an institutional practice. This is not to say there aren't solo practitioners. The demographics have changed. The law used to be restricted to white, WASP men of means in the U.S., and now women dominate, at least at the entry levels. The law has become diverse in race and socioeconomic status and increasingly in multi-disciplinary practice. The ethos of law has moved from a professional ethos, where lawyers set normative structure and enforcement, to one where rules are set by the market and the state.

How did the recession affect the legal industry?

The legal profession had been insulated by the large-scale trends that have transformed the rest of the economies around world. Now we're seeing these forces impact us, and lawyers are trying to figure out how to adapt. In general, lawyers have gotten away fairly unscathed after the financial crisis. Their day of reckoning will come when people ask what lawyers are responsible for. But even many business leaders escaped reckoning. There's been hue and cry but not a lot of legal repercussions. Lawyers are definitely taking a hard look at what the role of the legal profession was in enabling the conduct that we now think of as not good that led up to the crash.

What changes are happening in education in reaction to the marketplace?

It's responding to all of it. All of it is in flux. Tremendous change is going on. Legal education as a whole is trying to reposition itself. Legal education is becoming more diverse and has driven diversity in the profession. Law schools are trying to educate students in the competitive global economy while understanding the norms of the global economy. Legal education is itself a complex global player. It's changing radically around the world. The U.S. used to be unique in post-graduate, legal education, but now, more consciously, global law schools are prepping people for a more global understanding. There are, for example, the Peking University School of Transnational Law, the Bucerius Law School in Germany, and the Jindal Global Law School in India.

What does this globalization mean to students in law school?
     Working globally means you have to figure out where the growth of law is coming from. You better figure out how the complex systems of law that coexist interact. There is no global legal government or framework. There's a complex interplay between local, national, and regional organizations and norms of commerce. You have to figure out how to navigate this interplay and help your clients navigate it. This is increasingly common, even in family law. There are international issues in adoption, divorce, property settlements, custody, immigration, and trusts and estates. A lot of what lawyers do is a form of legal arbitrage. Lawyers look at competing legal regimes and evaluate how to position their clients to take advantage of these.

Is there anything to be gained in comparing legal education with medical education, which includes four years of graduate school and then additional residency programs?
     Many people think we should model legal education like medical education, with a general first year and then concentrations. At Harvard, we have concentrations. Many want to go further with formal apprenticeship models, but there is a lot of resistance to that model. The apprenticeship model has the disadvantage of depending on fixed categories. Once you're in a type of apprenticeship or residency, you rarely switch out. Specialization moves in one direction.
     That doesn't work well in the law, because, unlike doctors, lawyers may practice in many different areas throughout their careers. There is a tremendous movement of people throughout the practice areas. We interviewed 4,000 lawyers who entered the bar in 2000, and we surveyed them in 2003 and 2007 all across the

country. We found tremendous mobility. Almost half had changed jobs and sectors by 2003. Lawyers have to be flexible and mobile to adapt to the driving forces of their clients. So you have to teach lawyers how to move among these areas, not just specialize.

Will law school get longer than three years?

There is pressure to make law two, not three, years. For example, Northwestern is two years straight through. You might combine a course of legal study with undergraduate and graduate education to reduce the years of law school. We in the U.S. have much longer law schools than other countries, although school is lengthening in other countries. But then what do you do after law school? You can offer legal-practice training courses and formal and informal apprenticeships. The issue of the content of a profession comes up. Why are professionals considered professionals? There is a skill or trade dimension but also a broader set of normative and social functions. The concept of professionalization itself is under assault today.

Are you referring to the pressure on lawyers to structure their firms more like businesses?

It's more than that. This business pressure goes to the heart of what value lawyers have to offer. There is a problem with instrumental justifications for normative conduct when lawyers advise their clients about behavior the clients may or may not decide to engage in. Any good lawyer knows that while some behavior is legally permissible, you should still advise your client against it, because of other considerations: long-term reputation, the risk of liability, the risk of misjudging the line, etc. Being a professional means you have internal standards about proper professional practice. You do not just look to the marketplace for a measure of what's permissible from one moment to the next. It's about what it means to be a good lawyer.

Law schools today are faced with the challenge to define these professional standards in a world in which lawyers no longer have the luxury to determine these standards on their own. They are under pressure from client scrutiny, a more competitive environment, more transparency, and the increasing willingness of clients to shop among other lawyers until they get the answers they want. Yet if they give up totally on the project of defining professional standards, then they give up on the very thing that makes law a distinctive profession, and this defines their success. It's the paradox of professional distinctiveness. If lawyers succumb to the pressure to be like their corporate clients, they lose the very value that makes them lawyers.

Are law schools waiting to hear what's next?

There's a big energy around trying to figure out what's next, especially at conferences focused on the future of the legal industry. There is tremendous energy out there for reform. Some of the most interesting reforms are being discussed and experimented with not at elite schools but at those schools hit hard by the recession and hit hard by graduates who can no longer leave and make a living. There are not a lot of answers. You can talk to fifty people, and they'll all have their ideas. We are in many ways in uncharted territory.

In September of 2012, you participated in a task force in New York to discuss what the Wall Street Journal **called "the worst legal job market in twenty years," as a result of a study that found that nine months after graduation, only 55% of the class of 2011 had found full-time law jobs.**

The employment statistics are certainly sobering. But the Task Force's charge is to look beyond the current crisis to try to understand the underlying causes that will continue to reshape the market for legal services even after the job market improves.

In particular, how do we prepare students for the new kinds of law—and law-related—jobs of the next decades of the twenty first century? How do we prepare new lawyers for jobs in the corporate sector that will demand much more knowledge about the intersection of law, business, and public policy in an increasingly complex and interdependent global environment? How do we train lawyers who will serve individuals to provide cost-effective services that make greater use of technology, paraprofessionals, and directed self-help? How do we train government lawyers to understand and implement public policy in ways that maximize regulatory goals while minimizing its costs? And most importantly, how do we give tomorrow's lawyers the skills to move between these traditional careers in an increasingly dynamic economy?

To achieve these goals, we will have to be willing to rethink the role of both traditional legal education and the kind of apprenticeship and training that we have always expected the profession to provide in order to form a new and more effective partnership capable of working collaboratively together to train the next generation of lawyers. It's a big task, but with the caliber of people assembled on the Task Force, I am hoping that we will be able to begin to tackle these difficult but essential questions.

What new sorts of courses are you developing at Harvard?

The thing we're talking about in Future Education is that we have a new mandatory problem-solving workshop. We have a one-month, intensive January class in a workshop format, and we try to do three things. First, we introduce students to how real lawyers encounter legal problems. For example, we don't look at failed contracts disputed in appellate court, the way you would in a typical contracts class. Instead, we start with a client walking in with a problem or desire, and then: what next? We work from the bottom up with a strong attention to facts. Second, we teach students how lawyers work on legal projects, which is in teams. I judged a moot court in which students prepared a jointly written memo, divided work, and paid attention to productivity—just the way lawyers work in organizations or across organizational boundaries. Third, we introduce students to who lawyers are: a legal-services lawyer with a tenant-and-landlord issue; a big-firm lawyer considering whether to renegotiate a contract or sue; or a multinational corporation addressing child labor with third-party suppliers. The goal is to give students an introduction to the role lawyers play and to how to think about different situations that may or may not be legal ones. We think this workshop is a very important innovation in legal education.

What do the students say about it?

We've received very good student feedback. Students are uncomfortable working in teams. Many never had to do it before. The overall response is quite positive. We're convinced this is a key part of what the future of legal education is going to look like.

It sounds like a safe environment for students to try, make mistakes, learn, and try again.

This is their chance to figure out what they think. The stakes are higher in the real world. And speaking of the real world, television shows give people ideas about what lawyers do, and they're not true. There's a big mismatch between our cultural views of the law and the reality of legal practice. Law school is often a default education program. If someone doesn't know what they want to do, they go to law school. But then there's a lot of unhappiness when that kind of student finds out what lawyers really do. So this is a four-credit course on legal practice and how to survive as a younger lawyer. Students are asked to think about what they're going to do when a client asks them to do something they don't agree with or when a client asks them to take a position that's unjustified. Students learn not just what to do but how to say what they think.

Paul Smith

PARTNER
EVERSHEDS LLP
LONDON, UNITED KINGDOM

"Eversheds Consultants helps legal departments control their legal spend, improve compliance, improve the use of external law firms, benchmark other departments in other industries, and develop new revenue streams. We're helping GCs speak the language of management."

What moves did you make post-recession?
We, like other international law firms, were hit by the downturn in the economy. We had to do a lot of layoffs. We had a large real-estate practice, so we had to lay off staff there. Partner profits dipped 50%. By April of 2010, we recorded good results. We're optimistic we'll continue to have good results.

Is demand up?
Demand is up slightly. For big international firms, because of a shortage of mergers-and-acquisition deals, the market will be down. Litigation and regulatory are still strong areas. White-shoe firms have still done well, because big deals have taken place, but

middle-of-the-road deals have not taken place. Clients want 30% to 35% off the price, which is driving a lot of savage competition in the midmarket.

How are you delivering services?
There was certainly triage after the recession, but we've also moved to focusing on what we do best. We're looking at new ways of doing business, and the consulting offering is part of that development. We're looking at new revenue streams and new growth areas, and that's challenge for most firms. We're increasing our strong international coverage even more as our clients keep growing globally.

It's interesting how many U.S. law firms who have focused locally have awakened to the need for greater international coverage. My diary is full of meetings with U.S. clients and firms that are visiting London. We haven't seen that. They're trying not to lose their clients.

U.S. firms are trying to partner with you?
Yes. We have attractive international clients. Our strategy has been not to merge with U.S. or European firms. We have a strong U.S. client base. We have 500 U.S. clients, even though we're not in the U.S. Our policy has been to work with a small number of U.S. law firms rather than to merge. And, equally, if we had a client who wanted a U.S. listing, we could work with a U.S. law firm.

Does this arrangement enable flexibility?
Yes, and it gives us choice. There have been quite a few shotgun marriages between London and U.S. law firms. They may see some quick growth, but I'm not sure many of the transatlantic mergers have been thought through. In our case, we have good relations with a number of U.S. firms and direct clients, so there's no pressure on us to merge. We don't have many clients demanding we're in the U.S. They're demanding we're in China or Russia.

How are you dealing with pricing?
Pricing's tough, because clients are under pressure to reduce cost, and the market has reacted generally by seeking discounts on hourly rates, rather than trying other models out there in

alternative billing. We held an event in New York, and two-thirds of the delegates said they wanted to try alternative billing but felt they didn't have the tools to do so.

With alternative billing, you need to have a better handle on value for comparing services and performance. Discounting hourly rates is not the most effective way to reduce costs. As this area of alternative fees develops, I think clients will embrace the new models. Given the severe recession, people are simply using blunt instruments.

We do work for Jeffrey Carr at FMC Technologies. Jeff operates under what he calls the ACES model. The FMC in-house legal team rates the performance of outside counsel. We put in our bill for work we've done, and we're paid 80% of the invoice value. The rest of the payment depends upon feedback from the in-house legal team and the client. Under this model, we can get paid between 80% and 120% of the invoice value. With our relationship with FMC, we recover on average 10% more than the invoice value.

We find this a valuable way to deliver services. In all the best alternative-billing models, the firm has to put something at risk, which was never the case with hourly rates. The basis of workable alternative fees is that the firm and the client have skin in the game. We also do independent third-party client surveys, and our CEO sees the results of every client survey we do. Clients are constantly judging the performance of our lawyers, and that information is shared.

What about flat fees for a portfolio of work?

When we bid for Tyco's business in Europe, the Middle East, and Africa, they told us how much they'd spent in the last twelve months in Africa and Europe, and they said we would have to do all that work for 20% less in year one and 30% less in year two, which we achieved. That's a good way of looking at how we can drive down costs. You offer other law firms the opportunity to do the work of the last twelve months more affordably in the next. There is a huge reluctance among GCs to change law firms. In the recession, they've stuck with existing firms and sought discounts rather than move work to other firms at cheaper rates. During the recession, I've seen less RFPs than in the boom years, which suggests GCs are sticking with the same suppliers and driving down price rather than putting a book of business out to other firms.

Are the GCs going to have to drive the change to new models?

From my readings and conferences, I find a general consensus on the topic. The law firms have gone to the GCs and said, "Let's do it a different way. Let's use process efficiency, and we can cut costs." They offer a new way to do the same work, like document review, and save 50%. It hasn't been in response to GCs going to firms.

Maybe the GC community will force some change, but the real drivers of change will be CEOs and CFOs. Where we've been successful putting in new models, the impetus has come not from the GC (the Jeff Carr's of the world are unusual), but from the CFO telling legal departments to control costs and increase efficiency. And that's where our consulting business comes in.

How does consulting fit into Eversheds?

We officially launched Eversheds Consultants in September 2010. We spent quite a bit of time developing and testing the market. We have a team of twelve management consultants working within legal departments and helping them change. It's totally separate from the law-firm part. There has to be a split. We don't want to be seen as a consulting firm advising solutions that are always going to include using Eversheds lawyers. We sign nondisclosure agreements with our clients, because they're sharing information with us and don't want us passing that information to the firm.

What is your role?

I'm part of it. I lead on the development of business: creating new products, finding markets, and finding clients. Graham Richardson is the operations partner and leads the team to deliver the projects.

How did you develop the consulting business?

Working with Tyco and other company's legal departments, I've built up expertise and knowledge about how you put together new models for legal departments. I was acting as a consultant for clients with the intention of getting their legal business and feeling it was a conflict of interest. The clients understood it was useful to have the expertise, but the consulting model is to provide consulting expertise separate from the law firm seeking to win business. So what we've developed is a recognizable consulting business, the way consultants work in other professions, like accounting firms.

What are some of the things you help legal departments do?
We help them control their legal spend on projects, improve compliance, improve the use of external law firms, benchmark other departments in other industries, and most recently help them look at how they can develop new revenue streams. We're helping them restructure their internal department, come up with metrics, and speak the language of business. In a company, lawyers tend to communicate in Word, and everyone else in the business communicates in Excel. We go in and look at how they organize themselves. We use Lean Six Sigma to get the process more efficient. We look at whether they're getting good value from outside counsel. We're helping GCs speak the language of management.

This is what the CFOs are interested in. They don't want to see law as just a black hole of cost but as a way to generate revenue. Historically, in-house legal departments were meant to be reactive and keep clients from harm, whereas DuPont, for example, has been more aggressive in looking at getting money on the table. In-house legal departments haven't historically seen their jobs to be to go out and recover money, but now very often corporations have the benefit of contracts and intellectual property, and these haven't been actively pursued. With a recoveries program, you can look at what assets the company has. In five years, DuPont recovered $1.6 billion. (You can check out www.dupontlegalmodel.com.) They've transformed their legal department from a cost center to a profit center.

Are GCs willing to accept this kind of change from consultants?
We got a frosty response from many GCs a couple years ago, but now, with the pressure they're under, they're very interested in these programs. We are speaking to more CEOs than we ever have

before. I spoke at a conference for the CFOs of Global 100 companies, and the topic was transforming the legal department. They like the idea that a legal department can add to revenue. DuPont has been doing this for nearly twenty years, but finally, there's interest.

Is there interest in replicating DuPont's model?
DuPont was early. They introduced their model into the legal market in the late Nineties. They reduced their outside counsel from 430 firms to 30. They entered into closer relationships with those firms. They built the model around knowledge sharing. So firms shared knowledge. Now they have a model for information sharing, and the key word is *collaboration*. You only get that with trust. Amy Schulman at Pfizer has reduced the number of their outside firms, and she organizes teams made up of people from different firms. Lawyers may partner with their competitors and join forces for the benefit of the client.

Social media is a perfect way to increase collaboration. Lawyers have been slow to embrace the new ways, but technology provides many tools for collaboration. Virtual law firms want to save money and not purchase real estate, but their employees are, by definition, scattered. One of the challenges for virtual firms is making their people feel part of a larger whole. They work remotely, apart from an organizational culture. Social media may be one way to bring back a social cohesion.

What are the biggest trends that will affect how law firms change?
Nearshoring, legal-service providers doing more work up the value chain, and the rise of consulting. Another major area is social media, which will transform the way that everyone works and communicates with each other. I think the biggest pressure on major law firms is the cost of their real estate. They are tied into long leases with huge overheads. You reduce overhead by getting rid of real estate. You can work virtually. That's the next stage. You can reduce property cost by having less property, and the next stage is you work and communicate using social networks. We'll have fewer lawyers working in offices.

What new things are actually happening in the UK in the legal industry?

The hot topic in the UK is the alternative business structure (ABS), which is a licence you apply for to provide legal services. That began in April of 2012.

We have a statute called the Legal Services Act. It allows law firms to have external investors. With the classic partnership model, partners invest their own money or borrow money from banks, but the partners own the firm. Regulations have prohibited external investors. But with the new law, firms have already set up alternative business structures. One firm attracted forty million pounds of venture capital. Everyone is watching what's going to happen. The venture capitalists see law firms as attractive, because firms have big clients and big revenue.

Companies are also marketing legal services directly to consumers. People don't like going into lawyer's offices, but in the way that supermarkets have pharmacies and opticians, you might soon be able to go see a lawyer at the supermarket and buy a house, write your will, or organize your divorce while you're doing your shopping. All these new models will emerge as a result of the Legal Services Act. There's great anticipation to see who will succeed and who will fail.

What about consumers rating lawyers, the way they rate transactions on Amazon.com or services on Angieslist.com?

Yes, we're already seeing websites where people rate their experiences with lawyers. People in the UK are sharing horror stories on Solicitorsfromhell.com. That's only a short step away from Expedia and Trip Advisor. The Facebook generation has an obsession with sharing information. It's part of a trend toward greater transparency.

It's hard to make good judgments without good information.

And people want to understand each other. I'll sit with a client and bring in an expert partner on a topic, and the expert partner gives his views, and the client looks at me and asks, "Did you understand any of that?" The trend is towards better communication and better understanding.

And it's not just about getting rid of the jargon. I was trained in London, and when I was one week into the job, I had to write a letter to a client. I asked a colleague, "What do I do?" I researched the law, but I didn't know what advice to give. It's not just about jargon. It's about coming up with good advice.

Here's the best example that I give. A utility company called me about problems they had with an elderly couple complaining about the noise of their utility trucks going through the main gates at night. I sent a bright new associate to lecture the elderly couple on nuisance and common-law cases from the 1800s. But the client called and said an elderly lawyer had suggested just buying the couple double-paned windows for their house. Simple. It was not showing off knowledge of the law. It was commonsense advice.

A Note on the Project

David Galbenski and David Barringer collaborated on the book *Unbound: How Entrepreneurship is Dramatically Transforming Legal Services Today* (2009). After the success of that book, both Davids undertook a follow-up project: this book of interviews. The hope was that a book of interviews with leaders from all quarters would provide an up-to-date snapshot of the positive and dramatic changes taking place in the industry. The authors are grateful to the legal visionaries for fulfilling that hope—and then some. The legal industry is undergoing historic changes, and the authors thank all interview subjects for taking the time to contribute their remarkable experiences to this book.

David Galbenski

David Galbenski is an entrepreneur, lawyer, author, and public speaker with global reach. He is the founder and Executive Vice President of Strategic Initiatives for Lumen Legal.

His entrepreneurial achievements include being recognized as an Ernst & Young Entrepreneur of the Year Award Winner and being a two-time recipient of the Inc. 500 award, which celebrates the 500 fastest growing, private companies in the USA.

David is a passionate supporter of building the next generation of entrepreneurs to innovate and create products and services that help to solve some of the world's biggest issues. As the Global Chairman of The Entrepreneurs' Organization in 2008/09, he helped fuel the entrepreneurial spirit in over 40 countries around the globe.

His books include: *Unbound* (2009), *Rainmaking for Lawyers* (co-authored with Ridgely Goldsborough, 2012), and *Change Your Four-Letter Word Habit* (2013).

David graduated with distinction from the University of Michigan Business School in 1990 and *cum laude* from Wayne State University Law School in 1993. He currently resides in Grosse Pointe Shores, Michigan, USA, with his wife, Lynn, and daughter, Sarah.

Contact: dgalbenski@lumenlegal.com.

David Barringer

David Barringer is an author, designer, photographer, artist, and teacher. He has written a dozen books, including novels, story collections, and essay collections. He teaches graphic design, branding, writing, and more at the undergraduate and graduate level. He has taught at Winthrop University and the Maryland Institute College of Art (MICA). He has written for the *New York Times*, the *ABA Journal*, *Print*, *I.D.*, the *Detroit Free Press*, and many others.

David won the 2008 Winterhouse Award for Design Writing and Criticism, and his most recent collection of essays on graphic design, art, and design culture is *There's Nothing Funny About Design* (Princeton Architectural Press). He graduated from the University of Michigan (1991) and the University of Michigan Law School (1995). He may be reached at www.davidbarringer.com and dlbarringer@gmail.com.